"Emily is the big si͏  young women, I appreciate her a of her experi- ences. She is relat ;irls."

-Amber Lane

"Emily helped me uncover that hiding behind my daydreams is getting in the way of the dreams God has for me in the real world. She got right down to the point and left no room for me to hide from the grace God has given me!"

—Britney Monte, senior

"Emily knows what girls my age worry about—college, grades, who we're gonna marry—and she gives insightful advice with solid Scripture to back it up. Highly recommend!"

—Hannah Fulks, junior

"*Graceful* made me think about how much I want to be valued by other people. I realized that I don't need to do anything to be important because God made me in his image, and I have value because of him."

—Kylie Jones, senior

"Emily's book, *Graceful*, made me realize that I need to stop hiding my true self behind barriers I have built. I want to be more open to who God's made me to be, and what he has planned for my life—otherwise I might miss it."

—Rachel Walters, junior

"Emily gives real-life scenarios that girls like myself can completely relate to, and she helps guide us through the crazy emotions and doubts that we have in high school. She reminds us that God's plan for our lives is bigger than we are, and he is the only one who can really satisfy us!"

—Lupita Mendez, junior

"Youth leaders, parents, and mentors can say it over and over again—'Your value comes from Christ alone!!'—but the message just doesn't click for most teenage girls. Emily, on the other hand, gets right into their world and becomes their best friend. She walks them through her own story and instead of offering syrupy flattery and a high five, she convicts them with the hardcore Truth of Scripture. Because the Truth is, God doesn't take low self-esteem sitting down. It actually breaks his heart. He made these girls. He wants them to see themselves through his, their Maker's, eyes. And Emily will take girls to that place where not only will they start to tear down walls of guilt, insecurity, and self-doubt, but they will also discover a deeper love for Jesus Christ, their Creator and Savior, whose hands are strong enough to carry them through every self-loathing thought."

—Sarah Nutter, youth leader

"We all have a desire to be right with God that comes naturally. When we try on our own and strive to make ourselves right is when we get in trouble. Women of all ages struggle with this dilemma. How wonderful if young women would learn this lesson early and not spend their adult lives striving to receive the gift that has already been bought, wrapped, and given. Emily has done a great job walking through the book with us and helping us unclench the hand of striving and controlling and helps us open our hands to receiving the beautiful gift of grace."

—Jill Shelby, high school Sunday school teacher

graceful

(for young women)

LETTING GO OF YOUR
TRY-HARD LIFE

emily p. freeman

Revell

a division of Baker Publishing Group
Grand Rapids, Michigan

Published by Revell
a division of Baker Publishing Group
P.O. Box 6287, Grand Rapids, MI 49516-6287
www.revellbooks.com

Printed in the United States of America

Library of Congress Cataloging-in-Publication Data
Freeman, Emily P., 1977–
    Graceful (for young women) : letting go of your try-hard life / Emily P. Freeman.
        p. cm.
    Includes bibliographical references.
    ISBN 978-0-8007-1983-8 (pbk.)
    1. Young women—Religious life. 2. Self-perception—Religious aspects—Christianity. I. Title.
    BV4551.3.F74 2012
    248.8′33—dc23
                                                        2012013190

Unless otherwise indicated, Scripture quotations are from the New American Standard Bible®, copyright © 1960, 1962, 1963, 1968, 1971, 1972, 1973, 1975, 1977, 1995 by The Lockman Foundation. Used by permission.

Scripture quotations labeled AMP are from the Amplified® Bible, copyright © 1954, 1958, 1962, 1964, 1965, 1987 by The Lockman Foundation. Used by permission.

Scripture quotations labeled Message are from *The Message* by Eugene H. Peterson, copyright © 1993, 1994, 1995, 2000, 2001, 2002. Used by permission of NavPress Publishing Group. All rights reserved.

Scripture quotations labeled NIV are from the Holy Bible, New International Version®. NIV®. Copyright © 1973, 1978, 1984, 2011 by Biblica, Inc.™ Used by permission of Zondervan. All rights reserved worldwide. www.zondervan.com

Scripture quotations labeled NLT are from the *Holy Bible*, New Living Translation, copyright © 1996, 2004, 2007 by Tyndale House Foundation. Used by permission of Tyndale House Publishers, Inc., Carol Stream, Illinois 60188. All rights reserved.

Some names have been changed for privacy purposes.

The internet addresses, email addresses, and phone numbers in this book are accurate at the time of publication. They are provided as a resource. Baker Publishing Group does not endorse them or vouch for their content or permanence.

12 13 14 15 16 17 18   7 6 5 4 3 2 1

For the quiet girl who sits in the back, the loud girl who thinks she should be different, the girl who couldn't do it as well as her sister. For the daughter who just wants to please her parents, for the student who wants to do it right, for the friend who is always the smiling sidekick.

For the good test takers and the strict rule makers. For the athlete succeeding and competing, for the star. For the dancer and the painter and the daydream maker. For the worried and the hurried and the sweet smile fakers.

For the prom queen who cries in the bathroom, the artist who ignores the canvas, and the poet who never speaks up. For the girl who feels both too much and not enough.

For the girl who is tired of trying and the Christian who doesn't know Jesus. For the girls who win and the ones afraid to fail. For the pretty one, wondering if she's enough. For the smart one, worried on the inside. And for those who say *I'll be fine* and *I'm not lonely*—for the liars.

For the girl who knows everything and nothing.

For the rule followers, the fear wallowers, the messy, and the misunderstood. For the self-critic and the silent judge, and for those who feel invisible.

For the wanna-be leaders, the gonna-be women, the someday mamas, the soon-to-be world changers, and the present-day idea makers.

These words are for you.

contents

the beginning

Your ears will hear a word behind you, "This is the way, walk in it," whenever you turn to the right or to the left.

—*Isaiah 30:21*

The little white house on Gladstone Avenue had a driveway that ran the length of it on the right side. The gravel popped and crackled under the weight of any car coming through, sending up gray billows of dust. So we had some warning when Dad pulled his white Datsun up beside the house at the end of the day. It was the automatic *on your mark, get set* signal to my sister and me. We needed to get into position for a round of hide-and-seek.

Our house was small, and there were exactly three good hiding spots: behind the overstuffed recliner in the corner, behind the long curtains in the living room, or under the kitchen table. But anyone who hid under the table was nearly always found first, so maybe there were really only two good spots.

I still remember through seven-year-old-girl eyes: he walks through the back door in at the laundry room, and Mom hollers out a mom-ish

"I have no idea where the girls are" comment as she stands over the stove, stirring the chili. The pursuit begins. I have an overwhelming urge to laugh and wet my pants, and I hold myself into a ball and shake with excitement, both hoping he finds me and hoping he doesn't.

Dad knows all the good spots, but he plays along and looks everywhere else first, letting us girls win at our game. And if we hear his voice close to the place we are hidden, we wiggle and squirm and retreat deeper into our hiding. We get giggly, and the play goes on a little longer.

As I grew up, I stopped playing hide-and-seek for fun. Instead, I played for survival. When you're a kid, it's a game. As you get older, hide-and-seek can become a way of life, and you don't even realize you're playing it.

I've done a lot of hiding in my life, but not the kind of hiding you might think. I'm not a fugitive hiding from the law or a runaway hiding from my troubles. I didn't spend high school hiding boyfriends from my parents or pot under my pillow. I've never been suspended from school, stolen the answer key to a math test, or been drunk, high, or arrested.

My hiding was so clever that I had everyone fooled, including myself. The ways I chose to hide were not obviously offensive. I was nice. I was lovely and bubbly and likable. I was a good girl. But I hid myself behind my good girl image.

Like in my living room all those years ago, there are really only a few good hiding spots in the world, and we all compete for position behind them:

We hide behind our intellect.

We hide behind our sweet personalities.

We hide behind our rules.

We hide behind our comfort zones.

We take on different identities, often without realizing it. It's as if there are voices in our heads telling us who we are:

I'm the responsible one.

I'm the nice one.

I'm the smart one.

I'm the shy one.

I'm the worried one.

I'm the good one.

I'm the boring one.

We listen to these voices, and they drive us deeper into our hiding places. It may sound weird to call these hiding spots—*I'm not hiding*, you may say. *I'm just living. And I'm trying to do a good job of it. What's wrong with that?*

Well, nothing. Maybe. But it could be possible that you are a little bit like me—you're living life well; you're making smart, safe choices. But there is pressure, and because people seem to have high expectations of you and because your parents are so proud of you and because you want to do well so badly, success means everything. Failure is devastating. Weakness is unacceptable. Rather than letting people see your doubts, you hide behind a firm smile. Rather than risking rejection, you choose to keep your fears to yourself by pretending not to care. Rather than admitting you don't know what to do next, you fake it in public and feel lost when you're alone.

When you are a good girl, you move through life like a well-trained cheerleader, elbows and knees locked, smile on your face, standing on the sidelines. With your shoulders tense and your teeth clenched tight, you brace for tests and right answers and are ready for anything. You have a great respect for your obligations.

In a world where everyone's motives drip heavy with expectation, you wonder if anyone knows who you really are behind all that good. *Do they care? Do they see me over here, trying my best to do things right? Working hard to please them? Struggling to keep it all together?*

These outward identities we build for ourselves are not all that we are. A person is made of so many layers. Skin is just the top layer. It's the part you can see, so when you walk into a room, others won't run into you. It's the brown-hair, brown-eyes layer; the you-look-good-in-green layer.

Your outside is important because God made that part. He made you on purpose, uniquely beautiful. But you can't stop there, because that's your body, your skin, your outside. Dead people have all that stuff too. There's something else that makes you alive.

And so you keep digging and you see a little more. Maybe you laugh like your mama, talk with a hint of a lisp, enjoy country music, or put fries on your hamburger. Maybe you stay up too late at night and regret it in the morning. Something about a large moon in the night sky is comforting to you. You think about the future. A lot. You panic in the spotlight but crave it at the same time. You make friends easily, and you worry what they think.

Before you know it, you've gone deeper. You're starting to uncover what motivates you—the things you fear might come true, and worse, the things you fear might not. You have a longing to be understood, but still feel the need to protect yourself. You are happy, sad, scared, joyful, loved, unloved, rejected, and accepted all at the same time. And though you feel alone, so many of us feel the exact same way.

Your layers run deep. Most of life, we function on the top layers, the ones that show up in the mirror. The ones others can see. People like us or don't like us based on those top layers. They make judgment calls—and so do we, by the way, even though we want to be seen and known for who we really are. But who are we really?

This is a book about that.

This is also a book about God, about what it means—and what it doesn't mean—to believe. It might challenge some of the things you have come to accept as normal. Sometimes it might seem as if the words are written just for you, and they are. Other times it might seem as if you can't relate at all, and that's okay too, because that part may be for another girl—maybe even for a friend of yours. I simply ask that for the time we have here together, you would be willing to receive. I don't know what God might have for you exactly. But if he has something, wouldn't it be awful to miss it?

Consider the ways you might be hiding out, the things you are looking to for security and for safety. Perhaps we think we want to remain hidden, to keep to ourselves, to maintain our safety with our own hands. We have grown so comfortable in our girl-made hiding places that we forget the most important part of hide-and-seek: *the best part of hiding is being found*. If no one is looking for you, what's the point of hiding? Don't we all really want to be known, to be loved, to be accepted, to be searched for, to be found?

An invitation has been offered, but only the desperate can hear it. Dare to lift your eyes up from your books and achievements. Tilt your head toward the gentle whispers of a God who says, *What is it you truly seek?*

There are lots of answers to that question. Love. Money. Fame. Success. Beauty. Peace. Safety. Knowledge. Fun. Freedom. Perfection.

But all of these are secondary things. Because we were made in the secret, mysterious heart of God and anything less than God himself will always leave us wanting more. Some girls look to fill the emptiness with their rebellious ways and get into trouble. Other girls try hard to fill the emptiness with good things and get praise. But both girls are reaching for something we'll never find outside of God.

There is a different way to live, a way that is full of grace and mystery, a way that cannot be outlined or studied for or figured out.

Life isn't about trying hard to be good, it's about trusting God to be *graceful* in us.

When you hear that word *graceful*, maybe you think of something that moves in a beautiful or elegant way. Maybe you imagine a dancer on a stage or a bird in the sky. Lovely. Beautiful. Smooth.

In Christ, being graceful simply means *you are specially marked by God's divine grace*. In a very real way, this kind of graceful is also lovely and beautiful. His grace is a gift you don't deserve and can't earn. Because we are loved and known by a graceful God, we are free to relax our shoulders, unclench our fists, and open our hands to receive all he has to offer. And the best thing he has to offer is, quite simply, *himself.*

I know that's hard to imagine, in a way. Maybe you're wondering what it actually means to live a graceful life. We've got many chapters ahead to figure out what that might look like for you.

As we get started, there are two things you need to know about me. First, most days I still feel seventeen inside. I look around and wonder when the grown-ups are going to show up and take care of things, and then I remember I am one. We are not so very different, you and I.

The second thing is, I am emotionally allergic to small talk. I want to cut straight to the heart. I love to have fun and laugh way too loud, but my true passion is to listen to what is really going on behind those eyes. So when you read this book, know that I've done my best to cut out polite small talk. This is your invitation to be authentic. Take it or leave it, but don't talk about the weather.

the girl who wears a paper face

I'm too much but not enough all at the same time.

—Anna, a good girl, age 17

She didn't want to cry. As Kayla sat on the bed across from me at midnight, her tears were ready to fall right out, but she was fighting hard to keep them in. Our last session of the overnight youth retreat was finished, and I noticed her lingering in the background. Something was clearly on her mind. Rather than join the other girls, who by now were loud, silly, and sprawled out on pillows, she caught up with me. I could tell she was desperate for an answer but had a hard time articulating the question.

Finally, out it came. "I just want to make sure my relationship with God is right before I go to college," she said with a hint of urgency.

"Really?" I asked her, eager to find out what she meant. "What do you think you have to do to get it right?"

Kayla was the last girl in the world who should be worried about doing things right. She was a straight-A student, loyal to her friends, a generally sweet and sensible girl. Kayla knew what was right. Still, she answered with a sigh.

"I don't know!" Her frustration was evident.

I tried a different approach. "How will you know when it *is* right?"

She paused, considering the question. She didn't have an answer, but I didn't need one. The look on her face was familiar to me. In high school, I had often been overwhelmed with the feeling that perhaps I was missing a vital part of the Christian life. The question I constantly asked myself was this: *What am I supposed to do?*

How do I know I'm in God's will? What college should I go to? What should I major in? Who is it okay to date? What is it okay to do when we're dating? What is the right thing to say in this situation? Am I allowed to be angry/hurt/sad/annoyed?

What am I supposed to do?

If someone would have just made that clear, then I would have done it. I just wanted to know I was on the right track, and I didn't want to make any mistakes.

Maybe you want to know you're on the right track too. You may have accepted Jesus when you were five, been baptized at ten, gone to every Vacation Bible School possible, and brought twenty-five of your friends to church every week. Or maybe you accepted Jesus and then proceeded to walk in the opposite direction. Most likely, you find yourself somewhere in between those two extremes, somewhere in the middle. That's where most good girls live.

I've been a good girl all my life. And by that, I mean exactly what you think. I grew up going to church, Vacation Bible School, youth group, handbell choir, youth mission trips, a little bit of Young Life, and was even a member of the Fellowship of Christian Athletes, though the only time I met with them was for the yearbook picture.

I even had a good girl name, and I never liked it growing up: Emily Morland. It didn't roll off the tongue like other girls' names, like Sarah or Jessica or Ann. Mine felt more like peanut butter. During roll call, the M's fell right in the middle of the alphabet, blending in just like me. I had brown hair, too straight to be called curly but too curly to lay straight. I've never dyed it or permed it because I've heard it causes irreparable damage. So I've settled for brown. Mousey brown.

I have exactly one piercing in each ear. And only my ears. I don't have any tattoos. Needles.

I didn't sneak into R-rated movies, I didn't skip class except on senior skip day, and even though I did cheat on a few tests in biology, I felt super guilty about it. I didn't drink in high school because it was illegal and because I watched people throw up when they drank too much. And the only thing I hated more than breaking the rules was throwing up. But I liked having friends too much to skip the parties altogether, so I was the designated driver for my girlfriends. That got real old really fast.

I wasn't always a model good girl though. The first time I cussed for real was in gym class in the sixth grade. For all of fifth grade, Jenny and I were best friends. And then we got to middle school and she became friends with Natalie who, from what I can remember, wore glasses and scarves and seemed to have something against me. And so I did what seemed the natural thing at the time. I entered into the drama.

As I walked laps with a friend in gym class, I talked bad about Jenny, using some of those bad words that would have had my mom in tears. Just before we passed under the basketball goal, my tongue felt fat and clumsy as I said *the word*. I spoke it a little too loudly and my cheeks warmed at the sound of my own voice. I may or may not have begun to sweat profusely at the sound, but

I felt powerful. I felt big and believed in that moment that I was going to change my reputation. I didn't want to be such a good girl anymore. I wanted people to fear messing with me. I'm sure that was convincing with my mousey brown hair and my smaller-than-average frame, but I wanted to be intimidating. At least that's how I acted. The truth is, what I really wanted more than anything was to be liked. As much as I talked bad about those girls, I would have given anything for them to like me.

A few weeks later, something happened that I can't remember, but we talked. And we laughed. And before I knew it, Jenny and Natalie and I were sitting together at the lunch table as the best of friends. I was so relieved.

Wanting to Be Her

When I was in sixth grade, I wanted to be tough and untouchable, but really I was squishy and sensitive. In high school, I wanted to be unflappable and calm, but really I was easily hurt and just as easily excitable. I also wanted to be a perfectly disciplined student, but in reality I was plagued with an uncanny knack for procrastination and a tendency to cry under pressure. And if you turned on the interrogation light and gave me a truth serum to make me talk, I would tell you that I actually wanted to be perfect in every situation. I know it's impossible to actually be perfect, and I would never want *you* to be perfect. That's no fun, to have perfect friends. I want *you* to be imperfect and limited and relatable. But me?

I want to know what to do. I want to know how to do it right. And I want to do it. All. By. My. Big. Self.

Not only do I want to do everything perfectly, I want to look perfect while I do it. I want to act perfect and sing perfect and have perfect teeth. I want to speak perfectly and laugh perfectly and be clean and on time. Every time. It's ridiculous and embarrassing, but it's true and you don't even have to give me a truth serum for me to tell you that.

In the past, my solution to the giant gap between the girl I wish I were and the girl I actually am has been to somehow make my life look the way I want. I work hard to do the right thing. I stay strong when I feel weak, and I fake happy when I want to cry. My ideal image of myself has everything to do with put together and nothing to do with falling apart.

My friend Amber, a senior in high school, says it this way: "I am trying to work my way to my own happiness by trying to control the perception that others have of me. I feel like when I'm in control of it, then everything is okay."

Like Amber, I desperately want to manage your opinion of me. Nearly everything I do is to convince you I am good. If I sense that maybe you don't believe that about me, then I will do anything to change your mind. I want you to like me, and I will hide my real self so you can see what I consider to be my best self.

But you're a Christian! you might say. *Aren't you being kind of a hypocrite? Saying you trust God, but then acting so wimpy when people don't like you?* Honest answer? Probably. I'm not telling you this because it's a good way to be. I'm just telling you the way it has been for me.

This fear of rejection drives me hard, eating away at my courage. And so my love is cautious. My faith is timid. My story is small. I long to be seen, but I feel safe when I'm invisible.

So I stay a good girl.

And I hide.

I hide behind my good performance and my respectable reputation. I hide behind my sweet personality and my good intentions. For a long time, I even hid behind my parents' faith, believing it was mine. It kind of was, but it kind of wasn't. I was too scared to admit that. Overall, I hide behind busy and comfortable, and I work hard to manage everyone's expectations,

The energy it takes to live for you is killing me—to see me through your eyes, to search for myself in your face, to be sure you are pleased with me. I want you to always be pleased with me.

And then there is God.

I know God is big enough to save the unruly, the rejected, and the addict. I know about the God who reaches way down into the pit and the one who has love that stretches all the way up to heaven. But what about me, the good girl in the middle? Maybe he can't see me because my story is so boring. I lack intrigue, drama, and interest. Can he see ordinary, unspectacular me?

I'm not sure, so I vow to do everything right just in case that might help: to be a good girl, a good Christian, a good student, a good friend. I believe God will be more pleased with me, the girl who does it right, than he would be if I didn't. I try hard to measure up to what I think he expects, and I imagine him standing blurry in the distance, watching. It feels like God is far away, and so I practice the presence of fear and refuse the presence of Jesus.

I lived this way for many years. Sometimes even now when I forget the truth. Fear pushes and shoves me around. But what is the opposite of fear?

Courage?

Bravery?

Boldness?

Those all seem right. But God's economy suggests something different.

> God can do anything, you know—far more than you could ever imagine or guess or request in your wildest dreams! He does it not by pushing us around but by working within us, his Spirit deeply and gently within us. (Eph. 3:20 Message)

Fear pushes us around. But what God does in this verse—doing more than we could guess, working deeply and gently within us—to me it sounds a lot like love.

Things Most Girls Have in Common

While I've been working on this book, I've struggled with using the term *good girl* because there is a risk that as you read, you will get the wrong impression. You may tune out early because you're thinking in your head, *Well, I'm definitely not a good girl because of this bad thing I've done.* You may not relate to these words, but don't let that be because you've made mistakes.

For the purposes of this book, being a good girl is more about what you believe on the inside than how you behave on the outside. That means even if your story is very different from mine or from the other stories I will share, you may still struggle with this good girl in your head. If you have managed to live your life so far without getting into much trouble, the good girl in your head challenges you to work hard to keep it up. Or if you have made some wrong choices or messed up in small or even big ways, the good girl in your head will try to scold you and tell you that the answer is to get your act together, straighten up, be good.

Either way, the result is you depending on yourself to do life right. Either way, God isn't even in the room.

We all have at least some things in common: we feel the weight of holding it all together; of longings not yet met; of worry, anxiety, and fear about the future. And sometimes, if we are really honest, we wonder why we try so hard to follow the rules if all it gets us is more worry and anxiety.

When you are a believer in Jesus but you don't know what a difference he makes, then the natural thing to do is depend on the things you do know. To get you thinking about whether or not you struggle with this good girl identity, take a minute to put a check beside the statements you agree with. And if you are such a good girl that you can't bring yourself to write in a book, you can just answer these in your head.

___ I know how to be a friend and listen with interest.

___ I know how to get good grades in school.

___ I know how to get people to like me without doing anything wrong.

___ I know how to avoid conflict.

___ I know how to be a positive person.

___ I know how to fake nice when I feel angry or upset.

___ I know how to tell people what they want to hear.

We tend to put a lot of confidence in the things that are awesome about ourselves and try to hide the things that aren't. If Jesus fits in there somewhere, great. If not, oh well. But we will always run into problems living life that way, because when we put all our confidence in the things we know how to do, what happens when we encounter things we *don't* know how to do? Worse, what happens when the things we know how to do don't work? Put a check mark next to those statements that are true about you in the list below.

___ Sometimes I don't know what to say to my friends when they have problems.

___ I have cried about the pressure of school or homework.

___ I am devastated when someone doesn't like me.

___ I hate conflict.

___ I don't pray enough.

___ I don't really read the Bible, mainly because I don't understand it.

___ I don't think I measure up.

___ I judge people.

___ I compare myself to other girls.

___ I feel moody and irritable for no reason.

___ I snap at people.

If you are like me, you were able to check most if not all statements on both lists. How can it be possible that I know how to get people to like me and at the same time feel devastated when they don't? It's because even though I can be successful in my efforts some of the time, there is no way I can be successful all of the time. So where does that leave us?

It leaves us needy. I want to encourage you today: needy is a beautiful place to be. When we recognize our need, we will finally look around for something (or someone) to fill it.

For a long time, I have listened to the good girl voice in my head rather than the voice of God. In moments of brutal truth, I wondered if being a Christian was all about simply trying to be good. At times I knew that wasn't the case, but I couldn't figure out why my experience walking with Jesus seemed so hard.

I don't want to tell you what to do. Instead, I want to walk with you as you learn what God has already done. And I want to dare you to believe him.

Where the Hiding Began

There's a good reason why we hide. There's a reason why we long for perfection, why we want to have it all and be it all and experience life to the fullest. We were made for paradise. Truly. I'm not just making this stuff up.

"In the beginning, God created the heavens and the earth" (Gen. 1:1). Imagine the heavens and the earth without death, litter, pollution, poverty, power lines, exhaust pipes, nuclear plants, oil spills, parking lots, heart attacks, hurricanes, or graffiti. Imagine only deep blue skies, trees green and lush, every kind of flower you could dream up, and more. Imagine tigers walking tamely among sheep. Imagine a man and a woman existing together without argument, fear, insecurity, embarrassment, shame, or divorce.

God made this earth with his holy hands, and he made it perfect. And in the middle of it all, there was Adam and there was Eve, free and complete and unashamed. They were so beautiful. They were perfect. They were marked by God's grace. His favor rested upon them. Their lives were naturally graceful.

Everything God made was available to them. Everything, that is, except one tree. Just one. It was called the tree of the knowledge of good and evil, and they were told not to eat from it or they would die.

I'm sure you know the story, how a snake slithered through the branches of that tree while Eve stood close by. And he whispered doubt into her mind: *Has God really said you shouldn't eat from any tree in the garden?*

The truth is, God didn't say that at all. Twice he gave Adam and Eve guidance and instruction on what was theirs. First he said this: "I have given you every plant yielding seed that is on the surface of all the earth, and every tree which has fruit yielding seed; it shall be food for you" (Gen. 1:29).

And then he said again, more specifically this time, "From any tree of the garden you may eat freely; but from the tree of the knowledge of good and evil you shall not eat, for in the day that you eat from it you will surely die" (Gen. 2:16–17).

Do you see the subtle twist? We have an enemy, a real one, who takes what is true and twists it two clicks to the left so that *every tree but one* becomes *no tree at all*.

Like when I was a senior in high school and my parents gave me an 11:30 p.m. curfew and I would come home at 11:45 and they would be upset. And I was all, *It's not fair! It's only fifteen minutes!* And they would be all, *You've been out since five. What's fifteen minutes?* Instead of being thankful for the six and a half hours of fun I just had, I was mad about the fifteen minutes I didn't have.

Discontentment shows up when we focus on what we can't have rather than what we do have.

We have an enemy who takes a gigantic highlighter to the story of our lives and highlights those areas to remind us. Again and again. That's what he did with Eve in the Garden. There were thousands of fruit trees to eat from. Every tree was theirs. Except that *one*. The serpent wanted her to feel as though she was missing out, and he tempted her with something that was beautiful.

Fruit. It wasn't even dipped in chocolate or caramel. It was healthy. It was good for her. It was a good-girl-worthy temptation.

Sin didn't enter the world because Eve cheated on Adam with another man. It wasn't because she smoked pot behind the bushes. It wasn't because she and Adam had a fight or because she cussed out God.

Sin entered the world because Eve believed a lie about a piece of fruit. But it wasn't the fruit itself that caused the fall of man. It was what eating it meant. "The serpent said to the woman, 'You surely will not die! For God knows that in the day you eat from it your eyes will be opened, and you will be like God, knowing good and evil'" (Gen. 3:4–5).

I imagine in that moment, Eve began to feel anxiety, uncertainty, suspicion, and anger. *Perhaps God isn't so good after all. He is keeping something from us.* And so the serpent lied, the woman believed him, and she ate because she thought it would make her like God.

> When the woman saw that the tree was good for food, and that it was a delight to the eyes, and that the tree was desirable to make one wise, she took from its fruit and ate; and she gave also to her husband with her, and he ate. (Gen. 3:6)

Did you notice that Adam was with her? He wasn't across the Garden. He was standing right there beside her, and he did nothing. Eve didn't do this thing alone.

Then the eyes of both of them were opened, and they realized they were naked; so they sewed fig leaves together and made coverings for themselves. (Gen. 3:7 NIV)

They made coverings for themselves.

And there it is. They believed a voice other than God's, and they hid.

Satan attempts to recreate that scene every day of our lives. If sin entered this perfect world because a girl heard a lying voice and believed it, then no one can ever say that what we believe isn't important. What we believe is the most important, because what we do flows out of what we believe. Eve is the first girl to prove it, and we've been proving it ever since.

When we believe voices other than God's, we hide too. Adam and Eve started it, but we keep it going.

They hid because they were afraid.

They hid because they were embarrassed.

They hid because they were ashamed.

And so are we.

So there they were, sideways and upside down, the voice of their only enemy still echoing in their minds, and they got busy doing the only thing that felt safe at the time: hiding. The first hiding place was made out of fig leaves sewn together in fear and chaos with trembling hands and a mounting sense of urgency.

"They heard the sound of the LORD God walking in the garden in the cool of the day, and the man and his wife hid themselves from the presence of the LORD God among the trees of the garden. Then the LORD God called to the man, and said to him, 'Where are you?'" (Gen. 3:8–9). He asked, not because he didn't know, but because he knew the only way for them to truly experience life was to come out, to show up, to run to their Father and find their safety in him.

I'm tempted to think, *Well, they did the one thing God told them not to do. They deserved whatever punishment they got.* And it's easy to think that as long as I keep myself separate from the story. But another part of me recognizes myself in this woman. I am given the chance to believe God on a daily basis, and I continue to forget what I long to remember. And when I do, I hide too.

When we talk about this word *hiding*, it simply means this: anything I turn to in order to get my needs met. When I want people to think I'm smart, capable, and put together, I hide behind my performance. When I fear you will see what a mess I am, I hide behind my positive emotions. I hide behind my good reputation rather than risk trusting an unpredictable Jesus. I hide behind my list of rules so I can check off each one, as if I'm another step closer to God because I've followed them. I hide behind my strengths because I'm ashamed of my weaknesses. What started at the very beginning hasn't stopped yet.

As I sat on my bed with Kayla late that night, listening to the muffled laughs of the girls in the next room, the silence between us held an air of expectancy. I knew I should say something, and I was sure if I did, she would remember it. A question came to mind, and I knew it wouldn't have an easy answer. I asked it anyway.

"What if I told you the work is done? What if Jesus dying and then coming back to life was actually enough? What if you don't have to do anything but receive him, say thank you, and then live like it is true?"

The words lingered in the air between us. I watched as the tear that had been welling up finally made its way down Kayla's cheek. "That sounds good," she said, smiling shyly. I don't think she really believed me, but it seemed to be the best news she had heard in a long time.

In the following pages, I want to begin to change the conversations you are having in your head. Like me, you may want to know, *What am I supposed to do?* I want to introduce you to a different, better question: *What am I going to believe?* Every decision you make flows out of what you believe. I won't tell you what to do. I will tell you who to trust.

Each of the following chapters describes a different voice, and each voice takes on a sort of personality. To help you visualize the motives behind these voices, I've included a chart, "From Good to Graceful," in the back of the book that outlines each of these good girl voices—what she says, fears, and hides behind. Because you may not identify with every single good girl identity in the following chapters, this chart might help you sort out some ways you may uniquely struggle. It's tempting to believe these voices, to take them on and wear them around. But they are in opposition to the voice of God's Spirit within us. They do not define us, but they will direct us if we let them. And so we have some important choices to make. Every day, a direction. Every minute, a decision about what we will believe. Are you going to keep trying hard to be good on your own? Or will you dare to believe that you are graceful in Christ, marked forever by his divine favor?

the actress

Hiding behind Her Good Performance

God hath given you one face,
and you make yourselves another.

—*William Shakespeare*, Hamlet

During my second year of college, I decided I wanted to become a sign language interpreter. One of my required classes for that major was Acting 101, because so much of interpreting English into American Sign Language depends upon your ability to tell a story with your eyes, your face, your whole body.

In a sense, interpreters give up their own personalities and surrender to the personalities of the people they interpret for. If the English-speaking person is funny and dramatic, the interpreter signs funny and dramatically. If the English-speaking person is monotone and boring, a good sign language interpreter will show that on her face. She may not be fun to watch, but she will be doing her job well by interpreting not only the words but also the essence of what's being said.

So I took an acting class to learn the fine art of becoming someone else.

I loved it. Loved. It. And apparently I was pretty good at it, because my teacher pulled me aside after class one day and asked if I'd ever considered pursuing acting. I said no, and I hadn't, but I was always kind of flattered by the fact that she thought I was good at it. After graduation, I worked as a sign language interpreter for several years, and that acting class helped me to be a better one.

While acting served me well in my career, it did not do me much good in my real life.

When Good Things Turn Bad

My friend Kayla from the overnight youth retreat was trying to be the perfect Christian. She would have denied it if I had said it that way, but in essence, that's where her anxiety came from. She could feel her weakness and her lack, and she didn't like it one bit. Many people acknowledge they can never be perfect. They say, "I'm not perfect, so what's the point? I'm not even gonna try." Kayla and I did the opposite.

I said to myself, "I'm not perfect, so I'll try harder." Filled with determination and rules, I was ready to follow step-by-step to get life right, including my relationship with Jesus. I thought for sure I could figure it out if I tried hard enough, like algebra or driving or skiing.

If praying to receive Jesus was the starting point and seeing him face-to-face was the end, I wasn't sure what to do in the middle. I prayed. I read my Bible. But what I did best was simply *be good*. I desperately wanted to experience life with Jesus, but I didn't know how. I did what I could and hoped for the best.

I was addicted to perfect. And there is nothing more maddening than to be addicted to something you can never get your hands on. My addiction permeated nearly every thought and motive in my life.

Since I couldn't *be* perfect, I thought it would serve me well to at least *act* perfect. Not in a snobby I'm-better-than-you kind of way. It wasn't a thing I tried to flaunt like you would a diamond ring; it was more a thing I had to carry, like a bulky suitcase—less like a show-off, more like a slave. I felt the weight of impossible expectations, and maybe you can relate.

We are taught to perform. And we are taught to do it perfectly. It's almost like the whole world is rigged to get us to perform:

School	Hobbies	Jobs
Sports	Girl Scouts	Chores

Performing well isn't a bad thing. Doing your best is good and even necessary in lots of situations. When I got my wisdom teeth pulled, I paid my dentist to perform well. When you go to a movie, you expect the actors to put on a good show. When you go to Starbucks, they promise a perfect cup of coffee or they'll make another one. The best audition gets the part. The best speller wins the bee. We reward good performance with money and fame and reputation and attention.

It's no wonder we are so messed up when it comes to walking with God. In nearly every aspect of our existence, good performance equals good reward. Except not with him. A good thing turns bad when we perform to earn God's acceptance rather than simply receive it like a gift.

The Voice of the Actress

There isn't just one type of good girl. In some ways, I think every girl struggles with the voice of the good girl in her mind, whether or not she chooses to listen to her. We all believe somewhere deep inside that we should be better, be doing more, be someone other than who we currently are. Those are things the good girl says.

But there are different ways she shows up in us, different characteristics she has. We will talk about eight of them, and there are probably eight million more you could think of if you tried.

If there is any identity that most good girls can relate with, it's the Actress. It isn't that we are fake and pretend-y all the time, and it isn't that we are drama queens, although that could be part of it. What I'm talking about is the way we feel as if we aren't good enough. And so we *act* in such a way as to cover it up.

Imagine with me that you don't make the grade you wanted on a chemistry test. *I got a C? No good. I can't believe I made a C! I'm so stupid.* So I put on "stupid" as my identity and I begin to wallow in self-pity for an unreasonable amount of time.

That is when the Actress begins to speak. *Get your act together. Stay up until midnight or longer if necessary. Do whatever it takes to get it right.* On the outside, it looks like I'm working hard and being a good student. And I am. But in the realm of the invisible, I still believe I am stupid, so I perform to avoid looking stupid. I am not free.

I perform so you will like me. I perform so you will think I'm okay. I perform to prove my worth to you, to God, and to myself. I perform because I don't know how *not* to. I'm hiding in an unsafe place.

When rebellious girls perform to get their needs met, they get in trouble. When good girls perform for the same reason, we get praise. That is why the hiding is so easy for us. We work hard, we do right, and we try not to ruffle feathers. And it works! People like us, are pleased with us, and we do well. But what often happens is we are so focused on getting people to like us and be pleased with us, we don't really know who we are, and nobody else does either.

Part of the performance is healthy and right. We have to try on different roles, to playact scenarios and see which personalities fit and which ones don't. It's what we all do as we grow up. It's the way of things. But there is a difference between discovering your identity (who you are made to be) and creating a false identity (who you wish you were instead). The key to knowing the difference between these two identities is found in which voice you choose to listen to.

The Hiding—Listening to the Voice of the Actress

I never seriously considered being a rebel. I remember looking around the room at a high school party once, and I was the only one not drinking. I wondered why I felt so responsible and couldn't just lighten up and have some fun. But I didn't have it in me. There was too much at stake. I was good. I had a good reputation to uphold, a sweetness to protect, an important list of rules to follow, and a long list of people to please.

It was awesome that I didn't drink. Awesome. What is not awesome is that the reason I didn't drink was because of fear—fear of being caught, fear of what might happen, fear of what people would think, fear of getting into trouble. Being motivated by fear keeps a lot of good girls out of trouble. Because my performance was good and was praised by the adults in my life, I began to identify myself with that good performance.

My desire to be good protected me from a lot of heartache. I won't deny that. It protected me from pregnancy and bad grades and jail. But it did not bring me any closer to understanding God. And it didn't protect me from my own impossible expectations.

Growing up a good girl was exhausting. Good girls are good listeners. Good girls are always there for everyone else. Good girls don't get mad. Good girls are laid-back and easygoing. Good girls roll with the punches, go with the flow, follow the leader (as long as the leader is good, of course). I was a good girl and I wanted to be a good girl, but it often kept me from saying what I really meant. In fact, my desire to be good even kept me from exploring my own opinion, and I grew up to believe that my opinions didn't actually matter much anyway. I avoided vulnerability for fear of being rejected or being labeled as needy. Good girls aren't needy; they are need*ed*. And so instead of living free, I lived safe.

When we listen to this demanding voice of the Actress, our performance has everything to do with the Actress and her audience. She is constantly aware of herself and who's watching. For her, God is sitting out there in the audience along with everyone else. He's watching to make sure she gets everything right. And if she messes up, he might boo her, or worse, he might get up and walk right out of the theater.

The Finding—On Hearing God's Voice

If you are a girl who is hiding behind her good performance, it doesn't mean you have to start failing at everything in order to be free. But wouldn't it be nice not to feel the pressure all the time? Or if you could somehow escape the worry that seems to haunt you at night? Wouldn't you like to know for sure that the God who lives in the Bible can see you, here on a Tuesday in the twenty-first century? And wouldn't it be freeing if all of that could happen without your having to maintain and manage it all? That freedom begins or ends depending on which voice you choose to believe: the voice of the good girl Actress or the voice of a loving God.

In these pages, we are going to talk a lot about the word *receive*. Receiving the gifts God has to offer us can be difficult for the good girl. In this fast-paced, competitive, take-care-of-yourself life, it can be difficult to know how to receive things. It seems passive, maybe even selfish.

For a girl hiding behind her good performance, the concept of receiving could be somewhat foreign. She is more accustomed to giving, more comfortable offering herself to others, better at *doing*. But it is a beautiful, humbling thing to be able to receive gracefully.

Learning to Receive

Currently, I serve as a small group leader to ten crazy, fun high school sophomore girls. I've been with them for about a year now, and they continue to amaze me with their questions, their talent, and their heart. They are so beautiful, but I don't think they know it yet.

We meet every Sunday night in one of their homes, and one week just before Christmas, I pulled up in front of the house exhausted. I have three small children at home—twin girls in first grade and a son in preschool. They are fantastic, they are a gift, they are the joy of my and my husband's lives. They also need food, endless attention, and a bath sometimes. And so this particular night of small group, I pulled up in front of the house where we were to meet—tired, weary, and in desperate need of coffee. I sat in the dark for a moment, knowing the chaos and giggles were about to begin. I took a deep breath and opened my car door. Immediately, someone called out my name from across the lawn.

"Emily! Merry Christmas!" And before I knew it, two giddy silhouettes were hurling themselves toward me, their arms filled with bulky packages, their voices rich with excitement. As they got closer, I saw that they were carrying gifts. For me.

As we made our way inside together, the gifts kept on coming. Each girl had thought of me with a candle, a scarf, a plant, a drawing, a framed photo. I was overwhelmed. After all, they are in high school, and aren't high school students supposed to be selfish and self-focused? Isn't that what people always say? And even if their parents prompted them to bring me something, it still counts because they gave with such joy. These girls gave and blessed and thanked me that tired night in December.

But what if I had told them no? What if I had said to them, "You know girls, I'm good. I don't really need a scarf, thanks. I've already got one." How rude I would have been! How insulting!

When we receive a gift, we bless the giver. When we open our hands and take that which is offered to us, we are not only receiving the thing offered, but we are receiving the person. We say without words, *I accept you. I see what you have to offer, and I receive it with my whole heart. Thank you.* And we take it, and in so doing, we let the other person give.

We receive gifts from people all the time. We know how to do that. There is nothing you could ever do to make yourself worthy or deserving of what you've been given. And there is nothing you could ever do to make yourself unworthy. That's why it's a gift— because it's free.

One of the reasons I hid behind my good performance, one of the reasons I sometimes still do, is because I worry that I'm not doing enough, and because of that, I don't deserve the gift. I worry that *I am not enough.* But when I accepted Jesus, I didn't just receive a thing, I received a person.

There are many names for God in the Bible, names that highlight his different character traits. One name in particular bears significance for the Actress. God is called *El Shaddai*, the Hebrew word meaning "God Almighty, the God who is more than enough."

Jesus is a gift to us, and he is more than enough. Isn't that what we are longing to know? Isn't that what the Actress works so hard to try to prove or discover? You just want to know, *Am I enough?* When you received Jesus that first time at salvation, you actually received *the gift of enough.*

A New Kind of Hiding

It's good news to know we can't earn our own enough-ness. But it's a little bit uncomfortable, isn't it? Maybe you're thinking, *Um, that doesn't help me at all. I still don't know what I'm supposed to do.* Remember the better question: *What are you going to believe?* A girl who lives her life working hard and performing well would much rather be given something to do than be asked to simply believe. Belief is invisible and hard to prove. The hiding places offered to us by the voice of the good girl seem easier to take hold of: perform, work hard, achieve.

If life is like a movie script, the Actress is trying to write her own role, and she's exhausted. If you believe your role is to be the responsible good girl, then that is the story you will live out. If you believe your role is to be the polite, agreeable friend, then you will allow your script to be written by other people, and you may give little input. Or maybe you believe God wrote the role for your life, but it often feels like he is making you guess what your lines are. And you keep getting them wrong.

What if instead of trying to figure out how to live life the right way, you believe your life is more like a story *in progress*? And you and God are working on writing it together, today? What if instead of trying to play the role of the Actress, you received life as a gift and walked with God to uncover it?

We don't have to hide behind expected roles and scripts. We are free to listen to God and to live safely hidden in Christ. He gives us a better place to hide.

When we listen to the voice of the good girl, our God-given identity is hijacked by shame, and we try to perform our way out of feeling badly about ourselves. Choosing to bend your ear to the life-giving voice of God may look similar to listening to the good girl, but that is only from the perspective of an outside observer.

Let's revisit that chemistry test I mentioned earlier. I didn't make the grade I wanted, and I felt disappointed. I'm tempted to believe I am stupid. But the Spirit of the living, loving God whispers something different: *your grades do not determine your worth*. And so I have a choice to believe him and to receive my identity from him instead of from my performance.

Notice the event and feelings are the same. In both descriptions, the action is also the same—study hard for the next test. But there has been a shift in belief. And so there is a new hiding place. Now on the inside, instead of feeling tense, I feel free. Instead of holding so tightly to the outcome, I can know that God is with me in the process. Instead of working to be right on my own, I can choose to believe God is gracious toward me. He lives in me, and he wants to flow gracefully out of me in every situation. Even in my reaction to a chemistry test.

Whenever you hear a lying voice, there is always a true voice that speaks as well. The only problem is, the lying voice is louder at first because it usually comes holding hands with a feeling. It takes more work to hear the true voice, but that doesn't mean he isn't speaking.

Throughout these chapters, I'm not going to offer you formulas or lists. I'm not going to tell you what to do. I'm no good at that, and I wouldn't know what to say, anyway. Besides, if anyone was qualified to give a list, it's Jesus. But he doesn't make to-do lists for us, he offers *himself* and invites us to simply receive him, to remain in him, and to believe him. Are you willing?

Truths to Remember When the Actress Begins to Speak

God's script for you is personal. You do not have to keep up with, outdo, or become a better version of someone else. "You made all the delicate, inner parts of my body and knit me together in my mother's womb" (Ps. 139:13 NLT).

He will not leave you alone. You can rest in the presence of a loving Father who does not ask you to achieve but to simply receive the gift of his presence. "Do not be afraid or discouraged, for the LORD will personally go ahead of you. He will be with you; he will neither fail you nor abandon you" (Deut. 31:8 NLT).

The story ends well. You do not have to fear that it will all fall apart if you don't get it right every time. "'For I know the plans I have for you,' says the LORD. 'They are plans for good and not for disaster, to give you a future and a hope'" (Jer. 29:11 NLT).

the girl next door

Hiding behind Her Image

What a long time it can take to become the person
one has always been! How often in the process we
mask ourselves in faces that are not our own.

—*Parker J. Palmer,* Let Your Life Speak[1]

There's a game my friends and I used to play called *Would You
Rather?* Basically you have to choose if you would rather be one
thing or another, but you have to choose one and you can't be both.
*Would you rather be artistic or athletic? Would you rather be rich
or kind? Would you rather cure cancer or find love?*

During one game someone asked me, "Would you rather be
brilliant or beautiful?" I said brilliant, because *of course*. But I
was lying, because the truth is I wanted to be beautiful more than
anything in the world. I don't know where that came from; after
all, I wasn't exactly ugly. But I saw myself as just regular. Not

stunning and exotic like my friend Maria. Not gorgeous like my classmate Ashley Hall. I was just okay.

I really thought that if I were beautiful, I would never have any problems. It sounds ridiculous because it is, but that didn't keep me from thinking it. I imagined being able to walk into a room and make music with a flip of my hair, have every head turn, every conversation stop. I wanted to be captivating. I wanted to amaze.

As it turns out, my nose is a little too big for my face, my ears stick out a little too much, my eyebrows are straight across like caterpillars, and I have a lopsided grin. I tried to straighten it out once in the mirror, but it just confused me and made me cry. Not only that, my number one celebrity look-alike is David Schwimmer, and if the fact that he is a man isn't enough to convince you to be concerned for me, then you need to go look him up right now. (And while you're at it, go ahead and find out yours. You know you want to.[2])

Growing up plain in a small, southern Indiana town, there weren't a whole lot of ways to get into trouble. My sister and I spent summer days playing outside until the lightning bugs came out. We played Barbies and waited for pregnant cats to give birth to litters of kittens. We had lemonade stands but drank most of the lemonade before earning any money.

Our very loving and slightly overprotective mother had clear rules about things we were and were not allowed to do. We were allowed to walk down the back alley to Melissa's house as long as we stayed together. We were allowed to walk the half block to the convenience store for a Coke and a cherry Blow Pop as long as Mom was watching from the front porch. We were also allowed to ride bikes on the road as long as we stayed on the gravel shoulder.

We were not, under any circumstance, allowed to go under the bridge. That was where all kinds of awful happened. I never knew exactly what was so bad about going under there, but in the depths of my imagination I saw hordes of witches crouched in the dark, stirring their steaming brew, buying the souls of unsuspecting seven-year-old girls in cutoff shorts and skinned up knees. To go under the bridge was the ultimate declaration of independence from adult wisdom or supervision. To go under the bridge was to be a rebel.

Nearly four years older than me, my sister and her friends determined how the days would be filled. I got to tag along because I whined about it and Mom felt sorry for me. And one hot Indiana afternoon, we defied all wisdom, embraced our inner rebels, and ventured under the bridge.

I hate to say I don't remember anything about it. It was my big moment of rebellion, and my memory is blank. Once we got home my mind was flooded with guilt, canceling out any fun or adventure I may have experienced. Even at seven, I believed my role in the family was to be the good girl, the one who never got into trouble. And so I had an overwhelming compulsion to confess to Mom. I sat next to her, knowing I couldn't carry this heavy burden of my disobedience any longer. I purposely avoided eye contact with my big sister, who was across the room, boring holes into my head with her big, pleading eyes and tight lips, begging me not to tell.

I'm sure we were punished for doing something we weren't supposed to, and I'm also sure that I was less punished because I was honest and because I was younger. My poor sister.

My reaction to disobedience was just as it should have been: guilt. But that guilt was not a result of God's voice. I was simply a good girl with a heavy (and if you ask my sister, somewhat annoying) sense of right and wrong.

Even after I prayed to receive Jesus and was baptized at the front of that small church in the middle of a cornfield, that inner sense of responsibility continued to influence how I lived and the choices I made. Even though I was a believer, it didn't make a lot of difference in the way I lived. I was good before Jesus. I was good after Jesus.

And so it was that I continued with my good way of life, giving myself credit for all of my own goodness. There was a sense that

Jesus had something to do with it, as I clearly remember sitting on the playground under the monkey bars, telling my best friend about how Jesus died for her and all that. But I didn't understand the middle-of-a-Tuesday Jesus. I only knew him as a when-I-get-to-heaven Jesus. He was my ticket and not much else.

At thirteen, I "rededicated" my life to God because I was scared that perhaps it didn't take the first time. I stared at my feet as I walked up that orange-carpeted aisle and stood next to the pastor while all the grown-ups filed past with their pleased looks and proud words. All I could think was, *I can't wait to get out of here and what's for lunch?*

When Good Things Turn Bad

The Girl Next Door is a cultural stereotype for the all-American girl—the wholesome, friendly, regular girl. She's the type a guy is proud to bring home to meet his parents. She sounds pretty great, so what's the big deal?

Girls who make good choices throughout their lives are protected from a lot of junk. That is a good and beautiful thing. For example, there are plenty of books out there that warn you of the dangers and heartbreak of having sex before you're married. If you're reading this book, I'm assuming you've read some of those books or at least have a pretty good idea of what God's purpose for sex is.

But I want to share with you some things that can happen within those of us who are already making smart choices. Either (1) we don't believe our lives are very interesting, (2) we take all the credit for our own goodness, or (3) we feel responsible to keep it up. It's a different struggle than our rebel counterparts. While their struggles tend to be outward and obvious, ours are more inward and subtle.

Author David Seamands once wrote, "Children are the best recorders but the worst interpreters."[3] I remember a lot about being a kid. I remember colors and moments, arguments and smells, situations and conversations that are just as vivid as if I lived them yesterday. Though the images of the past are clear, the meaning behind them may or may not be.

So those feelings I felt after we went under the bridge that day are vivid and clear: *great recorder*. But the way I saw myself as a bad person and the way I scolded myself on the inside for making a bad decision: *bad interpreter*. The truth was, I disobeyed. But kids do that. It's how they learn. Yet even as a seven-year-old, messing up was not okay in my mind.

It works in positive ways too. I was praised a lot as a kid. My parents' friends and extended family members would comment on what a good girl I was, teachers boasted about my behavior in school, and I rarely got into trouble. I put a lot of confidence in myself and in my good reputation.

I was a good recorder of all that praise from the grown-ups who thought I was strong and capable. I remember their words and proud looks. I treasured their admiration. But instead of simply interpreting their words as encouragement, I internalized them and let them become a standard to continue reaching for. I put extreme pressure on myself to live up to the good girl in their minds. Even as early as elementary school, I wanted people to see me as able. I let their proud words define me, and it led to puffed up self-importance when I did well and devastating self-hatred when I didn't. If I was good, I got the credit. If I failed, I got the blame. There was little room for Jesus.

That's how the hiding works. Something happens that leads to a feeling, be it rejection or fear, elation or pride. And that feeling becomes a deeply ingrained belief. In turn, that belief turns into a way we choose to live and cope with things. What we do flows out of what we believe.

After all this talk about image, please don't think I'm asking you to try to change yours. Rather, I want to invite you to experience freedom from the heavy expectations that might be growing inside. We can spend a lot of time and energy building up our good reputations, making decisions that keep us looking good and right and honorable. There is nothing necessarily wrong with that.

Unless, like me, you begin to believe that your good reputation is the *goal*.

And you look at other girls who make different (worse) decisions, and you judge them.

And you feel better about yourself because of it.

The Voice of the Girl Next Door

Ashley Hall was the most beautiful girl in my school. Everyone knew it. She was arguably the most talented as well. She was a dancer, and in the small town where I went to high school, dancing was a pretty big deal. Years after we graduated, I learned Ashley ended up moving to LA where she danced in videos and toured with famous singers. No one was surprised.

I sat behind Ashley in algebra. She had white-blonde hair that looked whiter when it was dirty because she put baby powder on it. I remember someone telling me that at school, and I didn't believe them because I thought that was too weird. Until one day sitting behind her, I could smell it and see it. It was true. *Cool.*

I watched her during the two years we were in high school together. If we ever had a conversation, I can't remember it. She was gorgeous, slightly aloof, kind of royal. Ashley Hall had a great image.

Image is important to us. If you try to tell me it isn't, I will ask, when was the last time you took a photo down from Facebook because of that look on your face? When was the last time you looked in a three-way mirror when you tried something on? Only other people see you from behind. If you didn't care what they thought, why bother with the three-way mirror?

I look in the three-way mirror every time I try something on. It isn't wrong or bad to care what you look like. We all do. In fact, I think it is a good thing to care what you look like and value your appearance. I guarantee you Ashley Hall looked fantastic in a three-way mirror. Though her image was great, her reputation—well, that wasn't so great.

As a girl who accepted Jesus early on and pretty much did all the things I was supposed to do, I couldn't relate very well with the Ashley Halls of the world. In fact, I remember sometimes wishing I had the nerve to be a little rebellious. Then at least I would have an interesting and dramatic story to tell. I knew I was the kind of girl boys wouldn't try to mess with. They tripped over themselves to try to get the attention of Ashley Hall, but they didn't necessarily respect her. I was glad to be respected by the boys in high school. And when I say respected, I mean they didn't try to have sex with me. Ashley was the girl the boys wanted to be seen with Saturday night. I was the girl they sat with Sunday morning.

When Good Girls Do Bad Things

I am well aware that some of you may be able to relate more closely with Ashley Hall's story than you do with mine. Maybe you and your boyfriend have had sex. Maybe you messed up that one time last year and nobody knows about it. You've kept this secret from your parents and your small group leader and even your friends. And you think to yourself that if anyone knew who you really were, what you've really done, they would never accept you.

Or maybe you've messed up and *everybody* knows it. Maybe you have a bad reputation among your classmates and if anyone saw you reading a book about good girls they would laugh in your face because clearly, you aren't one.

I will repeat what I said earlier in chapter 2: being a good girl is more about what you believe on the inside than how you be-have on the outside. That means whether you've messed up big or you've messed up little, *we all mess up*. And in some ways, we are all haunted by the good girl voice in our heads. Some of us may be better at living up to the good girl expectations than others, but the point is, that voice tries to convice us that the way to fix ourselves is to try to do better, be better, look better. *But that voice is wrong.*

The answer for all of us is the same, no matter our reputations. Trust Jesus. Lean hard into him. Know that even if nobody else knows how bad you've messed up, he knows. Know that your brokenness does not repulse him, it attracts him. Know that the best we can come up with on our own is merely a heap of ashes. Whether your ashes are a pile of good works or of bad decisions, it's all ash. And he came to make it beautiful.

> To all who mourn in Israel, he will give a crown of beauty for ashes, a joyous blessing instead of mourning, festive praise instead of despair. In their righteousness, they will be like great oaks that the LORD has planted for his own glory. (Isaiah 61:3 NLT)

He loves you, wants you, picks you,
Anything good about you comes from him.

The Hiding—Listening to the Voice of the Girl Next Door

My own personal goodness is not a safe place to hide. But I didn't understand that at the time. Instead, my good image and reputation was where I began to place my identity. The wholesome Girl Next Door emerged from within, motivated at first by fear. Slowly though, it began to pay off. I was the girl who did things right; the friend others came to when they needed advice; the girl on the outskirts of drama; the sensible, cheerful one. My goodness became part of my identity. Soon, boys liked me *because* of my good reputation. The right kind of boys.

I got my braces off the spring I turned sixteen. It was the happiest day of my life. I drove home in my little black Chevy Spectrum, the car with no A/C or heat, and I swear it was made of plastic—the cheap, thin kind, like a Barbie car without the stickers. But one thing it did have was a working tape player. And when you're sixteen with straight teeth, that's all you need.

On my way home from the orthodontist, I rolled my window halfway down (if you rolled it all the way down, the driver door would swing open, a fact I discovered in a most dangerous way) and sped down the winding, two-lane back roads of Columbia, South Carolina. The bagpipe and the strange, haunting, offbeat rhythm of Peter Gabriel's "Come Talk to Me" filled the car as the wind pushed heavy past me.

I felt free, invincible, and in control. And all I could think about was that boy. He played baseball and had blue eyes so clear I could see all the way to the future. I cannot explain to you how hard I fell for this boy. He also had major high moral standards. He didn't party like the people we hung around, but he still managed to fit in with them. They respected him for his moral rightness, just like they respected me. He was my first real boyfriend, and I was sure we would be together forever.

We didn't drink or party or make fools of ourselves. We didn't tear one another down or fight or yell. We didn't have sex or anything close. We made good choices and our relationship was sweet and innocent.

We were right to not drink under age and to avoid having sex before we were married. But my reason for avoiding those things had little to do with responding to God and everything to do with impressing that boy. I had a reputation to maintain as the good girl. Because so much of my identity was being built on the foundation of my good reputation, there was a lot at stake if I slipped up.

So I didn't slip up. I was a well-adjusted, confident, healthy girl on the outside who was desperate for male attention, affirmation, and love on the inside. I looked to my boyfriend to satisfy my God-breathed longing for acceptance. I had my first glimpse of what it might feel like to be loved in a romantic way. It didn't take long for me to become addicted to that feeling.

We were created with a deep need for love, acceptance, worth, and security. The need is overwhelming and must be satisfied. While some girls hide behind promiscuity in their grasping for connection and acceptance, as good girls we depend on our good reputation to meet our desperate need to be loved. This relationship was a significant source of acceptance for me and began an unhealthy pattern of looking to boys to affirm my identity.

And so the things I believed as I listened to the voice of the Girl Next Door shaped my life, for better or worse. My boyfriend and I were not having sex, and so I felt proud of that fact. And it's okay to be proud of yourself, unless the pride leads to believing you are better than everyone else. That kind of pride leads to judgment, a job reserved for God alone. Instead of resting safe in a grace identity that comes as a gift from the hand of God, I rested in the seeming safety of my own good decisions. The problem? I was always just one bad decision away from an identity crisis.

The decision was good: not having sex with my high school boyfriend. All of the invisible ugliness and pride in my heart was not good. I heard the cautionary whispers God would offer to me as I lay awake in the dark: *Trust in me, daughter, not in your own good decisions. Come to me. Rest in the strength of my presence. Only I can meet your needs.* I chose to ignore his voice, shutting out my true source of acceptance and listening instead to the voice of the Girl Next Door.

When the boy's family moved away later that year, I was devastated to my very core. I don't remember anything about that summer because I existed in a lonely fog of memories, longing, and rejection. My source of value and worth had packed up and moved across the country.

Austin Carty was a contestant several years ago on the reality show *Survivor*. He's from my hometown and was invited to speak to our youth group one night. You know how the show works: twenty or so contestants are stranded in some remote tropical location and divided into tribes. They compete in challenges, and every three days someone gets voted off. The idea is to outwit, outplay, and outlast your fellow contestants. Whoever is the last one standing wins a million dollars. And of course, it is all recorded for television.

It was Austin's opinion that his fellow contestants' motivation for staying on the island in the midst of such harsh conditions had a lot less to do with the money and a lot more to do with the cameras. He believed that if the contest was exactly the same but not televised, most of the contestants would quit the first week. He may or may not be right, but it raises an interesting point. In his opinion, people care most about other people's impressions of them, even more than a million-dollar prize.

My reputation was my number one purity motivator in high school. The summer after ninth grade, my girlfriends and I met a guy named Tim at the beach. He was the hottest of his three friends, so naturally all of us were drawn to him. He was flirty and great at using cheesy pick-up lines, and even though we probably wouldn't have let him get away with that back home, everything is different at the beach. And so we laughed at all his jokes and thought he was fantastic.

He was a little older than us, and I distinctly remember sitting next to him on the steps of the pier, me on his one side, one of my girlfriends on his other. We laughed and joked as his hand rested inappropriately high on my leg. And it didn't make me uncomfortable. Wanna know why? Because we were at the beach. And we would never see this guy again. And whatever we did here, nobody at school would find out. And if the opportunity presented itself, if I found myself alone with Tim, I would totally make out with him. I wouldn't have sex because that was wrong, but anything else was fair. That's what I thought.

Thankfully, nothing ever happened with Tim. Three days after I met him, another boy showed up and he became the object of my short attention span. Yet later, those thoughts I had scared me. Maybe my convictions about my own purity ran only as deep as the impressions other people had of me. The next year when I dated the good boy back home, I was also good because that was what was valued.

In case you haven't figured me out yet, I was a little boy crazy in high school. Maybe you are much more sensible than I was, but I just couldn't seem to keep my mind off of those boys. Being boy crazy looks different for some girls than it does for others. Even if we aren't having sex with our boyfriends, it's still easy to find our identity in them in an unhealthy way.

I thought having a good reputation was one of the most important things about being a Christian. In Philippians 3:1–11, Paul describes his own reputation in great detail. He was circumcised on the eighth day, he came from the nation of Israel, of the tribe of Benjamin. He was one of the best Hebrews, and he was righteous and blameless in keeping the law. He had an impeccable reputation in nearly every area of life—religiously, politically, even genetically. And do you know that was even before he met Jesus? You don't have to know God to have an impeccable reputation. But do you know what Paul says about his good reputation after meeting Jesus? "But whatever things were gain to me, those things I have counted as loss for the sake of Christ" (Phil. 3:7).

The Finding—On Hearing God's Voice

Character is about who you are. Reputation is about who people *think* you are. I have cared more about who people think I am than who I really am.

Consider Jesus. He was not a person who tried to keep a good reputation intact. He never tried to explain himself for the sake of his image. In fact, when I began to notice the reputation of Jesus, it completely undid me. If I lived in Jesus's time, I don't think I would have liked him very much. My mom would not have let me hang out with him. He was way too scandalous and controversial.

In his book *Breaking the Rules*, Fil Anderson talks about the scandalous reputation of Jesus.

> He breaks all social etiquette in relating to people. He acknowledges no barriers or human divisions. There is no category of sinners he isolates himself from. Simply stated, Jesus is a miserable failure at meeting religious people's expectations of him. He connects with the kinds of people he should disregard. He attends the wrong dinner parties. He is rude to respected religious leaders and polite to whores. He reprimands his own followers and praises outsiders and riffraff.[4]

Jesus stirred things up wherever he went, and the Pharisees hated the fact that he existed. He associated with adulterous and unclean women, lepers, and tax collectors. Though he was without sin, there were still those who questioned his reputation. Knowing there were people who disagreed with and even hated him didn't cause him to change one thing he did. He wasn't working to maintain a good image, he was walking in dependence on his Father. Jesus didn't value what people thought; he valued people, period.

If you are able to make it through high school with your reputation intact, I want to offer you a most sincere congratulations. It will not come easy. It is a hard-won victory, complete with battle scars, broken hearts, and lots and lots of difficult choices. You won't always be able to avoid catastrophe and also keep all your friends. That can be a hard reality to accept. The girls who used to share your convictions are different now and you don't understand how you got here. They've changed and you have too, but their changing is away from you, away from God, away from what you used to share together.

But don't allow your coming away unscathed and un-pregnant trick you into believing that you can handle this life on your own or that you are somehow better than anyone else. Remember the layers we all have; don't get stuck on the top one. Your girlfriends who are living differently than you have the same layers you do, but theirs may be hiding deeper down. They are wounded and so are you. The way you choose to deal with the pain is different, *but it's all pain.*

My good reputation quickly became a sneaky hiding place, a pretty bubblegum place that kept me separated from "them." Our good reputations and Girl Next Door images can become little castles we build to stay safe. We look at the world from our princess towers, eyeing the dragons in the distance, thankful we've escaped their fiery mouths. And we should be thankful. But Ashley Hall was a girl just like me, hiding behind her reputation. We each put our confidence in the image we built with our own hands. Her reputation didn't look so great; mine looked fantastic. Jesus looks past both of those masks and just sees our hearts.

My good reputation isn't the goal. The goal is love. First, receive God's love like the gift that it is: free and un-earnable. Then, pour it out all over the place. Love and grace outweigh a thousand good reputations. Jesus lived a perfect life on earth, but his perfect life never built a wall between him and anyone else. When he was with people, he didn't focus on their behavior because he knew their hearts. And he knows our hearts too. Aren't you so glad?

A New Kind of Hiding

We are incapable of keeping ourselves from feeling prideful or judgmental or better-than. If you don't believe me, try it for a day or so, and you'll see. As soon as you think you've got your pride under control, you realize you are feeling prideful for controlling your feelings of pride. It's a gritty and vicious cycle. So what are we to do? The only thing we can do—receive from Jesus. Practice thankfulness for the discernment, for the faith. It's a gift, not a medal. It's a grace, not an award. And only through a daily belief in Jesus alone can the events of my life take on a different tone than before.

When you choose not to have sex before you get married, you may experience pride in that. As you depend on Jesus, that pride melts into thankfulness because you recognize that God is the one protecting you. As you believe his truth, you are able to love others. And you no longer find your safe place in your own good decisions. Now your safe place is found only in Jesus.

Remember this: behind the skinny actress with the Oscar win; behind the joke you think is stupid; behind the girl with the reputation that is falling apart in public; behind the tears of the girl being bullied and the harsh words of the mean girl who bullies her; behind the woman at the Food Lion who scans the cereal and the man sitting in the Oval Office—behind all of those images that people craft for themselves, there is a person, seen by God, created in his image, and longing to be loved and accepted. Just like you. No matter what their reputation, no matter what image they so desperately want to show you, there is a person. Don't forget to see them.

Truths to Remember When the Girl Next Door Begins to Speak

God is the keeper of my reputation. I do not have to make it my goal to please everyone around me. "For am I now seeking the favor of men, or of God? Or am I striving to please men? If I were still trying to please men, I would not be a bond-servant of Christ" (Gal. 1:10).

My goodness comes from him alone. I cannot manufacture my own goodness. All good things are a gift, and I am simply to receive them, say thank you, and then live like God is true. "Every good thing given and every perfect gift is from above, coming down from the Father of lights, with whom there is no variation or shifting shadow" (James 1:17).

He will defend me in times of trouble. When my reputation is in question, I have only to look to Jesus. I can run freely into his loving arms, because he is my defender. "One thing I have asked from the LORD, that I shall seek: That I may dwell in the house of the LORD all the days of my life, To behold the beauty of the LORD and to meditate in His temple. For in the day of trouble He will conceal me in His tabernacle; In the secret place of His tent He will hide me; He will lift me up on a rock" (Ps. 27:4–5).

the activist

Hiding behind Her Causes

*To be entirely honest, I know of nothing quite
so boring as Christianity without Christ.*

—*Major Ian Thomas,* The Indwelling Life of Christ

My friend Hannah looked forward to spending a month in Uganda. As a college student uncertain of what she wanted to study in school, the opportunity to serve with her two best friends on a mission trip was welcomed.

Now more than ever before, students are aware of the injustice in the world. Like Hannah, you want to do something about it. I absolutely love that. I believe God absolutely loves that. It's where his heart beats.

But like anything else, whatever we do—even good things—out of our own strength, or just because we think we should, can easily become another place where we try to hide, a place we run to for acceptance, worth, and security. We think being a good Christian means making grand gestures with our lives, big statements of service and activism and rescue missions. The Activist sits beside us, tempting us to save the world. There is always more service to volunteer for: wells that need digging, meals that need serving, people who need homes. And the Activist will tell you to save the world yourself instead of showing the world the Savior.

When Good Things Turn Bad

When Hannah left for her trip, her motives felt mixed, even to her. The Activist sat on her shoulder, repeating the list of all the things that would help her to become a better person: *travel to a foreign country, visit orphanages, feed hungry children.* Hannah felt the weight of these noble expectations in her soul, and she desperately tried to live up to them in her experience.

> Two days into the trip, I was exhausted. I was pouring out and trying to love, and I was spent. I loved them out of only myself. I loved them thinking I could change them. I loved them thinking my life would be changed if people saw me in dusty clothes holding little babies with sweat dripping off my brow.

While on the trip, Hannah realized the depth of her own inability and came to a place of great peace as she discovered the freedom that comes from serving out of God's strength rather than out of her own. She had a peace that seemed unshakeable. That is, until one hot afternoon while preparing lunch with her friends.

The Voice of the Activist

As Hannah and her friends made egg salad from some old ranch dressing, two of them made an announcement that shook Hannah to the core: "My two best friends announced to me that they sensed God was calling them back to Uganda. That once we left this place and went home, they would be coming back to stay." In that moment, Hannah's peace evaporated like water on the hot pavement outside. Because she didn't feel called back to Uganda; she felt called home. Boring, plain, familiar home.

Hannah did not feel free to share what she was really thinking with her friends because it seemed so un-Christian.

Really, God? You are calling them to use their gifts in a different country? That's the best thing you can do as a Christian. How come I can't do that? Am I not good enough? Do I suck at life? Is that why you won't let me do this amazing thing? So, for the next few days that was my thought process. Not to mention the fact I was alone. I couldn't talk to them about how I was sad. How I wept in the shower. How it felt like I was losing my best friends to God's calling in Uganda. They were going to leave me. Me. Me. Me. Me.

A few days later, while standing in the bug- and gecko-infested shower, Hannah heard God whisper into the deepest, most insecure parts of her soul: *Hey. Come here, my sweet, weary friend. Let me carry those burdens for you.* As she held a soapy loofah and watched the water and red dirt swirl around her bare feet, Hannah realized that God is not confined by geography, and he cares about her life and purpose more than she does.

It was like listening to a song that you've never heard before, and you want to listen to it on repeat for the rest of your life. As we arrived back in the States, I had to beg Jesus to sing me that song back again, over and over. We got back. We spoke at church. They said through tears they're going back. I said through tears I'm staying. I'm going to graduate. I'm going to help old people get hearing aids. I'm going to stay a receptionist. Most of us operate on an ordinary level. But we have an extraordinary God.

Though she still battled feelings of guilt, frustration, and sadness about the ordinary life she seemed called to, Hannah felt confident in the Lord's love for her and in the fact that he knows what he is doing. Even more, she felt sure that he is able to do great things through ordinary people.

It can be easy to confuse a calling to a people or a place as more important than a calling to intern at a radio station for the summer or babysit the kids down the street. Is Christ not present everywhere? Can he not work in our midst?

The presence of Jesus in the daily minute has the potential to cause everything we do to be supernatural. If what you are called to feels less than extraordinary, there is a tendency to think, *Well, the Lord has big plans for me later*. And you wait patiently until he decides to reveal that master plan. But what if his plan for you is right where you are? Are you missing it because you are looking for something *more* extraordinary?

The Hiding—Listening to the Voice of the Activist

A couple of sisters named Mary and Martha lived together in Martha's house in Bethany, a town in Israel two miles outside Jerusalem. Jesus and his disciples were traveling through Bethany and passed by Martha's house: "Now as they were traveling along, He entered a village; and a woman named Martha welcomed Him into her home" (Luke 10:38). Martha genuinely wanted to have Jesus there in her home. She was an eager hostess, and her motives started out right, as those of a good girl often do.

But once he came in, Martha began to worry. When God sits in your living room, a girl can get a little flustered if she thinks too much about it. And so while Mary chose to sit and enjoy the Lord's company, Martha chose to work hard and quickly grew frustrated. "Martha was distracted with all her preparations" (Luke 10:40). She knew this was a big deal. She knew this was important. But instead of enjoying the presence of Jesus, she worked hard to serve an elaborate meal.

Martha has a reputation for having her priorities out of whack, but I can't help wondering why people give her such a hard time about it. She could have been out partying with the people in the town and never even seen Jesus come by. She could have hidden out in the backyard until Jesus left, never inviting him in to begin with. She could have let the neighbors feed him. There were lots of other, worse things she could have been doing. But she invited him in. She wanted to give him a great meal. She wanted to serve him in the way she knew how. Why isn't that enough? Martha was a good girl!

I can so deeply relate with Martha. I know how to point out the bad decisions of people around me. *Well, at least I'm not doing what* she's *doing! I'm trying to do the right thing, the good thing, the best thing.* Still, it doesn't feel good enough.

What more could Jesus want from us? We don't party on the weekends, at least not like those other girls; we raise money for causes; we feed people who have no food; we wear pink on breast cancer awareness day; we like important movements on Facebook; we sit with the new kid in the cafeteria.

Martha, for one, wondered what more he could want, and she wasn't afraid to tell him so. "Lord, do You not care that my sister has left me to do all the serving alone? Then tell her to help me" (Luke 10:40).

I love this about Martha. She didn't hide behind her servant mask to suffer as a silent martyr. She could have faked happy until Jesus left and then blasted Mary for her lack of help. She could have given Mary the silent treatment for days after that gathering. There is nothing like a good dose of passive aggression toward a sister to get your point across. Or she could have kept all the anger and resentment to herself and then talked about Jesus behind his back, secretly blaming him for allowing Mary to be lazy while she did all the work. That's probably what I would have done.

But Martha didn't do any of that. Instead, she immediately took her frustration to the one who she knew could do something about it. "Lord, do You not care that my sister has left me to do all the serving alone?" And if that weren't brazen enough, she added, "Then tell her to help me." It's bold, rash, and embarrassing, Martha talking to God this way. But her honesty paved the way for Jesus to speak to her.

As it turns out, there *was* more Jesus wanted from Martha than her hard work and her righteous behavior. And there is more Jesus wants from me. Just like Martha, I have asked the Lord why it seems he doesn't even notice how hard I'm working, how much I'm doing for him. Why does he seem so hard to please?

In that question, I reveal a deep misconception I have about God. It isn't about what we are supposed to *do*; it is about what we choose to *believe*. While Martha was working hard to please God, Mary was willing to trust him. Jesus points out the difference: "Martha, Martha, you are worried and bothered about so many things; but only one thing is necessary, for Mary has chosen the good part, which shall not be taken away from her" (Luke 10:41–42).

Martha was worried about so many things, and so am I. I worry about doing enough, about being enough, about what people will think. I worry about the future, and I fret over the past. I try hard to do the best, to be the best, and I never feel like I really measure up. I have so many things.

Martha had many things too. One of her things was to work hard—maybe too hard? Perhaps she was naturally gifted as a servant, but she mistakenly thought her service was the most important thing.

The Finding—On Hearing God's Voice

I was scared the summer I turned seventeen, worried that moving to Detroit would be my undoing. I was the new girl from the

South, the one with the tanned skin who said *y'all* instead of *you guys*. It was fun to be new, because you have a little bit of control over your own awesome. And you can sort of start to believe that you really are who they think you are. At least for a little while.

I jumped into that small Christian school with everything in me, maxed out my schedule with advanced placement classes, served on a senior leadership team in my youth group, showed up early every Sunday night to pray with a few other students, worked at a camp for practically no pay. I worked hard that year. I was tired that year. But I was trying to be a good girl and a good person, trying to be the best I could be for God and for me and for everyone else.

Two years later, I was back in South Carolina for college and had just finished my sophomore year. I was preparing to transfer to another school but stayed in South Carolina that summer, squeezing out a few more months with friends before I had to move. It was a humid, sunny day as I sat in the living room of the old duplex I was subletting, my feet bare on the hardwood that never seemed clean no matter how much I swept it. I had my Bible in my lap, the one with my name written in swirly gold letters on the green leather cover, and I read a verse with the word *grace* in it. I don't remember which one.

All I know is, the verse troubled me. I felt like I knew a fair amount about holiness, about rules, about discipline, about faithfulness, about service. But I didn't really know about grace. I had heard it was amazing, at least that's what the song said. I knew I believed in it. I knew it was something good. But for me that day, something was missing.

I watched as those five letters seemed to float up off the page, demanding my attention: G-R-A-C-E. Being a good Bible college student, I looked up the word, what it meant, where it came from, the context, the background. With furrowed brow and unsettled heart, I couldn't get it out of my mind. I knew grace existed. Don't we all know that? Maybe. I don't know. Maybe not.

As it turns out, understanding grace doesn't come from study. It comes from need, and I'm talking more than just a need to know. Even so, I began to study this thing called grace. I read about it. I listened to recorded sermons about it. I prayed about it. I took classes about it. For the next several years, this concept of "undeserved favor" came up again and again. I didn't know at the time how trying to learn about grace would be like trying to straw-sip the ocean.

I believe this was the good part Jesus was talking about with Mary. She sat at his feet. She soaked in his presence. She didn't try to put herself behind a cause that would make her worthy of his attention. She didn't try to figure him out or reduce her relationship with him to an activity. She received him into her living room, and she allowed him to receive her, just as she was. That's grace. That's the good part.

Jesus may not walk down our neighborhood street the same way he did in Bethany, but we may welcome him into our living rooms in all kinds of ways just the same. It could be simply sitting with your little sister on her bed because she just found out that boy she liked doesn't like her back. It could be responding to your mom the first time rather than waiting for her to get mad. Sometimes it might look like service, but other times it might not. It might not look grand, and there may not be recognition for it.

The voice of the Activist tends to make sweeping statements that sound great: *You have to make a difference. You have to find a cure. You have to raise the money. You have to save the world.* But our identity doesn't come from being the Activist. Our identity comes from Jesus. It is amazing what can happen when we let go of our own expectations of service.

A New Kind of Hiding

I saw true poverty for the first time when I was invited to go with Compassion International to the Philippines. I had walked through the streets of my own town in the past, served meals to the homeless, seen the men on the street corners with the cardboard signs. But it wasn't until I got on an airplane and flew twenty-four hours to the Philippines that I saw the kind of poverty where entire families live on less than a dollar a day, where children walk barefoot through malaria-infested waters, where babies die from preventable diseases.

A few weeks before I left for my trip, people had all kinds of nice things to say to me—things like, "You are doing a good thing" or "Keep up this good work you're doing for God" or "You're so brave to go." If I didn't know better, I would have thought I was something special for saying yes to this trip across the world, for being willing to walk the dirty streets of Manila and sit in the broken-down shacks of the people there. But seeing this poverty does something to you.

I looked nineteen-year-old Michelle in the eye, the girl who lived in one room with her parents and three siblings, and I thought *I'm not the brave one, you are.* She isn't brave just because she is poor. She is brave because, even though she lives in poverty, *poverty doesn't live in her.* Because of Jesus, she found hope. And seeing her, I stopped looking at me. We both looked at Jesus, because he is the only hope. Not just for her but for me too. That's what service does. It points us to Jesus, not to ourselves.

In John 15, Jesus talks about what it means to live in a dependent relationship with him. He says he wants his joy to be in us and that we are to love each other as he loves us. And then he says this: "Greater love has no one than this, that one lay down his life for his friends" (John 15:13).

Sometimes it's easier to pick up a cause than it is to lay down your life.

Responding to God might be traveling to Uganda to work in an orphanage or raising thousands of dollars to build wells in Nigeria. It also might be sharing your textbook with that girl who sits behind you in calculus and doing it with a heart in love with

Jesus. There is no activity that is somehow more Christian than another. God looks at the heart, and that is the good part that Mary knew. He simply asks us to come as we are and to be willing, open to receive whatever he might have for us this day. That is what it means to be in relationship with Jesus. That is what it means to live a graceful life.

Truths to Remember When the Activist Begins to Speak

My competence comes from God, not from what I can do for God. "Such confidence we have through Christ toward God. Not that we are adequate in ourselves to consider anything as coming from ourselves, but our adequacy is from God" (2 Cor. 3:4–5).

Worship is the good part. God desires for us to trust him, not try to please him. "You are worried and bothered about so many things; but only one thing is necessary, for Mary has chosen the good part, which shall not be taken away from her" (Luke 10:41–42).

God does not boss you. When God speaks, there is not duty and obligation but lightness and joy. "These things I have spoken to you so that My joy may be in you, and that your joy may be made full" (John 15:11).

the heroine

Hiding behind Her Strength and Responsibility

You're blessed when you're at the end of your rope.
With less of you there is more of God and his rule.

—*Matthew 5:3 Message*

Alcohol was like the fifth member of our family while we were growing up. Technically, it was just my mom, dad, sister, and me. But my dad drank too much, and alcohol was so present in our lives that it seemed like an older brother who was around before we were even born. He wasn't the kind of brother who looked out for me in the halls at school. Instead, he completely ignored me and didn't even seem to know I existed. Alcohol is only friendly to the addict.

Beer cans stayed crushed under the driver's seat of my dad's white Datsun, and every time the car stopped at a light, they would roll out from underneath. My sister and I would push them back under with our flip-flopped summer feet, tin crunching against tin and sometimes pinky toes. It was normal to have a dad who didn't go to church, who didn't read us stories, who drank at dinner. And before dinner. And sometimes after.

He was an alcoholic.

Someone once told me that cardinals were good luck, and so every time I saw one of those little red birds, I'd wish for my dad to accept Jesus. Every falling star, birthday candle, and fountain penny wish was for my dad to know Jesus. Well . . . that and a ten-speed bike, but whatever.

My dad quit drinking the year I turned eleven. There was no Jesus moment, no support group. He simply quit. Knowing what I now know about alcoholism, that is nothing short of a miracle. He also began to show slight interest in the Bible and would occasionally go to church with us instead of staying home and listening to Bruce Springsteen turned up loud in the living room. I dared not hope for him to accept Jesus, until one afternoon in our Iowa basement when he asked me to tell him a Bible story.

When Good Things Turn Bad

It is a good thing to long for someone to know God, to pray for their heart, to ask for their eyes to open. But if you have a parent, friend, or other family member who isn't a believer, then you know the pressure that comes when they ask you about the Bible. It's like everything has been leading up to this moment. Every wish I had ever made about my dad's eternal salvation was converging here in front of me on this very important Saturday morning. Every hope for him to know about God seemed to rest on my skinny, jammy-wearing shoulders.

I completely blanked. I thought of what I had learned at Vacation Bible School over the years, but instead of the stories about Jesus and love and the cross, all that came to mind were visions of lemon-flavored cookies and Kool-Aid in small, flowery paper cups. And just when I nearly gave up all hope, a little tune began to weave its way to the surface of my memory. Before I could stop myself, out it came:

> Zacchaeus was a wee little man, a wee little man was he.
> He climbed up in a sycamore tree for the Lord he wanted to see.

I tried to speak it in a normal voice, tried to hide the fact that it's actually a song. He didn't say much after that, but he smiled and nodded his head. I walked up the stairs to my room feeling like a failure, overwhelmed and discouraged.

The story ends well, as it wasn't long after that day in the basement when my sober dad accepted Jesus as his personal Savior, no thanks, I'm sure, to me or Zacchaeus. But even though his salvation story was a life-changing event, it did not change the beliefs that were already deeply ingrained in me: *I felt responsible for my dad's salvation.*

The Voice of the Heroine

Being strong and responsible are not bad things. Doing your homework is the responsible thing to do. Telling the truth, loving your siblings, driving the speed limit, and doing chores—all good, responsible choices. These are not necessarily the things I'm referring to when I talk about hiding behind your strength and responsibility.

Instead, the voice of the Heroine twists these noble desires into something deeper, more heavy. When we listen to her voice, we are tempted to believe that we have to be all things to all people, have to make everyone happy and everything around us okay. And in doing so, the word *responsible* takes on a much bigger meaning.

re·spon·si·ble: liable to be called on to answer; liable to be
called to account as the primary cause, motive or agent; being
the cause or explanation[1]

I considered things to be my responsibility that were never meant
for me. I falsely believed that *I* was the cause or explanation for the
bad, uncomfortable, or dissatisfied people or circumstances around
me. Likewise, I felt the need to prevent the bad, uncomfortable,
or dissatisfactory circumstances from ever happening in the first
place. I needed to be the Hero, or since I'm a girl, the Heroine.

Do you feel responsible to be right, to look good, to have it all
together? Maybe you feel responsible for being responsible, which
means:

- being four years old and eating peanut butter and honey even
  though you hate it, just because your friend is eating it and
  you don't want to trouble her mother.
- being thirteen and the third best friend of two fighting girls
  who both tell you their side and feeling overwhelmed with the
  middle-ness of it all.
- being fifteen and watching your parents fight, knowing there's
  nothing you can do to make them love each other again.
- being seventeen and getting accepted to the college your entire family has gone to and not wanting to tell them that you
  don't want to go.

The even uglier side to this is that for all the times I rush around,
both physically and mentally, trying to fix and influence the people
and circumstances in my life, I also feel angry and resentful that I
am the one who has to manage it all. *Why doesn't anyone else fix
this? Why does it always have to be me?*

People go their entire lives carrying the burden and blame for
things over which they have no control: the death of a friend, their
parents' divorce, car accidents, natural disasters. But death and

tornadoes aren't the only uncontrollable phenomena. Really, all things are outside of my control, even though it doesn't always look that way.

I wonder if I'm doing enough, saying just the right thing, handling life the way I ought to be. I don't want to carry the heavy load of this strength and responsibility, but when I listen to the voice of the Heroine, I don't see any other option. If I let go, then what will happen?

The Hiding—Listening to the Voice of the Heroine

The summer before ninth grade, I was still soaring from having made the B-team cheerleading squad. B-team was a big deal. It meant we got to wear our uniforms to school and decorate the football players' lockers on game day. Somehow, I was voted captain of the squad, a fact I loved for all of eleven minutes. That's about how long it took for me to realize that being captain was a big responsibility.

To me, being captain meant I was supposed to know everything. So when we had to come up with a dance to perform at camp that summer, instead of asking for help from one of the other cheerleaders, I made up the dance myself. I found my favorite dance remix version of "Everybody Dance Now," popped the tape into my red boom box, and worked late into the night.

As it turns out, being able to dance is very different from actually making up a dance. I cannot begin to tell you how little I knew about choreographing a dance. But I was captain! I felt responsible. I falsely believed that since I was in a role of leadership, I was automatically supposed to know things. To ask for help would be admitting weakness, perhaps causing someone to think I wasn't qualified to be captain, which to me at the time was the worst thing imaginable. So instead, I hid my lack of knowledge, put on my mask of strength, believed the voice of the Heroine in my mind, and forged ahead.

The next day at practice, I taught that ridiculous dance to my squad. They learned the whole thing, bless their spunky little hearts. For a short time, I thought perhaps I had pulled it off, had uncovered my savant choreographing talent. But then we performed it in front of the varsity cheerleaders, the girls who looked like movie stars. To this day, I can still recall each girl by name because that is how much I looked up to them.

They watched as we "danced," and after telling me that my coolest moves were illegal in cheerleading, they did the worst possible thing they could have done in that moment. They laughed. And not the ha-ha, that-was-cute-but-let-us-help-you sort of laugh that you can join in on and pretend maybe you were kidding anyway. No, this was the lip-biting, pretending-to-cough, won't-make-eye-contact, whispering sort of laugh—the kind where you get dizzy-hot and wordlessly pray for death or a sinkhole or an invisibility cloak.

That was the last time I made up a dance on my own. It was also one of those defining moments, the kind that begins to shape you, for better or worse. I had to learn to ask for help after that. I also had to learn that hiding my weakness is often worse than sharing it ever would have been, even in something as small as making up a cheerleading dance in the ninth grade.

Listening to the voice of the Heroine feels right at first. She sounds so noble! So strong! She can handle this, right? Sometimes she can, and that gives us confidence to trust her again. But her ultimate goal is to mask the weakness, to hide what she cannot control, to appear stronger than she feels. The Heroine tells us we have to know everything, and when we don't, we have to hide.

The Finding—On Hearing God's Voice

There is an intimate beauty to be found in admitting you don't know everything. There is freedom, the kind you feel when you let go of the rope after playing tug-of-war. When my friend Faith and I went to New York to see *Wicked* on Broadway, we stayed with some friends living in Brooklyn. One night before dinner, we decided to head across the bridge into Central Park and ride one of those horse-drawn carriages. As soon as I settled into the seat, squeezed between my college girlfriends, the first thing I did was plop my heavy, touristy bag on the floor of the carriage.

Imagine this with me: what if I had continued to wear that bag on my back? My friends would have said, "Girl, take a load off. Put that pack down and enjoy the ride!" And what if I would have said, "Oh no, y'all. I can't do that. I wouldn't want the horse to have to work so hard."

They would have called me an idiot because, duh, the horse was already carrying the load. No need for me to carry it too. But heroines don't want to be high maintenance. We don't want to be seen as needy or weak or unable to handle things. As a result, we live life like a girl carrying her own pack on a carriage ride. God is already carrying your load. Why do you insist on carrying it too?

As good girls, we carry the weight of things that belong to God alone. Consider eleven-year-old me, believing that it was my responsibility to share the perfect story with my dad so that he would believe in God. God doesn't ask us to change people's lives; he simply asks us to live ours. Not in order to figure out how to *do life right* but to learn what it means to *live life well*. And he will do remarkable things when we live our lives as though we really trust him.

I can't help but think of young Mary in the Bible, doing her thing, engaged to Joseph the carpenter. She thought she knew how her life would go. She had plans to follow and dreams to discover. Until one day, completely unexpected, an angel showed up to speak with her.

We've heard the story so many times that it may seem tired and ordinary. But Mary was a real girl, engaged to a real guy, living a real life. She did not know how this story would end, but she knew enough about the Storyteller to trust.

When the angel tells her what was going to happen—that she had found favor with God, would have a baby and call him Jesus, that he would be God's Son, that his kingdom would have no end—Mary does not listen to the good girl voices.

She does not listen to the Actress and respond, *Okay! I'll work hard to be good enough to deserve being the mother of the Lord.* She had already found favor with God.

She ignores the Girl Next Door and does not try to manage her image or reputation. She does not say, *What will people think of me, being pregnant and unmarried?!*

She does not hide behind her causes and listen to the voice of the Activist. *But Lord! Pregnant? I was going to do such great things for you, but now I have to take care of a baby? What a waste!* She accepts this change of plans as from his hand.

She does not try to be the Heroine and hide behind her strength and responsibility. *Lord, I can handle this all by myself. Thanks for the challenge.*

Instead, Mary believes the voice of God. She trusts that God will carry the load of all those worries that rise up to the surface. And her first response is to receive his word as truth. "I am the Lord's servant. May everything you have said about me come true" (Luke 1:38 NLT). She was available. She was willing. She was graceful. She was in a position to receive her identity from God and no one else.

Remember, Mary didn't know how the story was going to end. She had troubles of her own, don't you know. There were many things she could have begun to list out, reasons why it was not okay for God to interrupt her life in this most unexpected way. She didn't know she would be bringing up this baby only to have him die in the prime of life. She didn't know he would be killed on a cross in the most embarrassing, horrific, criminal way possible. She didn't know he would come back to life and save the whole world.

But she knew one thing: it was not her job to be the hero. It was her job to trust the One who is, and to simply tell him yes. There is an important difference between *me doing the work* and *me trusting God to do the work in me*. Mary trusted God. She believed the angel, and then she offered herself as a servant.

The voice of the Heroine tries to convince us to hold on to control in every situation, to manage every event and person around us. God is not welcome to interrupt the life of the Heroine. She has her schedule planned out. She does not like disruptions.

What if Mary had listened to this good girl voice? What if she had believed that her plan was better than God's? What if she had said no?

I'm so glad she didn't say no. We know that meeting was planned from the very beginning, assigned not by the calendar but by the One who made the day and the night and called them good.

God does not ask us to carry burdens. He does not ask us to save the world. He does not ask us to come up with a plan. He simply asks us to *come*.

A New Kind of Hiding

In his book *Reflections for Ragamuffins*, Brennan Manning says there is more power in sharing our weaknesses than our strengths.[2] As a good girl, I have a hard time with that one, especially if it means other people might think I don't know everything or that I don't have it all together. The truth is, admitting weakness is the doorway the Lord uses to lead the tired good girl to a place of rest.

Three years ago, my friend Kendra and I were both leading high school small groups, and we began to notice evidence that the girls in our groups were listening to the voice of the good girl in a major way. It was easy to spot, as she and I both have spent the better part of our lives living behind the mask of strength and responsibility. We decided to take action and organize an extended time for some of these girls to hang out together and chat it up about Jesus, life, and the masks we hide behind.

We chose a Saturday in January to invite the girls for an overnight gabfest. There were twenty high school seniors hanging out on my living room floor, forty eyes darting around wondering if it was safe to come out. As we began to share with them our own messy stories of trying to measure up, of failing to trust Jesus, and of longing to be free, the air in the room shifted from reserved to relaxed.

Then, it happened. One brave girl stepped out from behind her strong exterior to share things she feared and ways she struggled. Heads nodded all around, tears collectively threatened to spill over from understanding eyes, and the girls began to trust each other. We couldn't have stopped them from sharing even if we wanted to, because Brennan Manning is right: *There is more power in sharing our weaknesses than our strengths.*

The power doesn't stop there. Even though it's freeing and relieving to share our weaknesses with one another, sharing alone won't bring much relief in the long run. Once we admit we can't control every circumstance or make everyone like us, then it's time to transfer our trust in ourselves to trust in another. And I'm not talking about accepting Jesus. Lots of Christians live their whole lives as believers, but they never truly learn what it means to trust God. We may be able to hide some of the mess from each other, but we have a God who sees and knows and loves anyway. Our generous, patient, compassionate God is crazy about you. His expectations of you are not the same as your expectations of yourself. Are you willing to release yourself from being the Heroine and trust him to be your Hero?

Truths to Remember When the Heroine Begins to Speak

You don't have to be the strong one. God does not ask you to come up with a plan. He simply asks you to come. "Come to

Me, all who are weary and heavy-laden, and I will give you rest. Take My yoke upon you and learn from Me, for I am gentle and humble in heart, and *you will find rest for your souls*. For My yoke is easy and My burden is light" (Matt. 11:28–30, emphasis added).

You don't have to figure things out. It feels risky to let go, but we are in desperate need of someone to depend on other than ourselves. "You're blessed when you're at the end of your rope. With less of you there is more of God and his rule" (Matt. 5:3 Message).

Learn the beauty of smallness. Sometimes the bravest and strongest thing we can do is to admit that we are afraid and weak. "And He has said to me, 'My grace is sufficient for you, for power is perfected in weakness.' Most gladly, therefore, I will rather boast about my weaknesses, so that the power of Christ may dwell in me. Therefore I am well content with weaknesses, with insults, with distresses, with persecutions, with difficulties, for Christ's sake; for when I am weak, then I am strong" (2 Cor. 12:9–10).

the bystander

Hiding behind Her Comfort Zone

Silence isn't the absence of God hearing, but
rather the sound of Him listening.
—*Holley Gerth,* God's Heart for You[1]

When I went to college, I started out as a piano major. My freshman year, I tried out to be the accompanist for a singing group that traveled around the region. I got the part, but that wasn't saying much as I was the only contender. It was nerve-wracking work, and I wasn't prepared for the pressure. The pianist holds the whole performance together. If she falls apart, so does everything. I fell apart a few times during performances. I wasn't confident enough in my piano skills to remain in the spotlight, and I didn't love it enough to get better. That was when I changed my major to sign language interpreting.

As an interpreter, it was basically my job to blend in and be invisible. I was much more comfortable with that than with being a piano accompanist. Every day I interpreted what one person said to another person and back again. My voice did not have a say in the matter. It was actually my job to not have a voice. I simply showed up, day after day, and interpreted words and meanings from one language into another.

I am a lover of words, and so there were ways in which it was a fascinating job. But in other ways, it was a job that kept me on the sidelines. I didn't have to have an opinion about things; I got to express other people's opinions. Sometimes that was fun, like when the hilarious history teacher would tell stories to the class and I got to be the one to deliver those stories to the Deaf students. Other times it was not so fun, like when the teacher would disrespect the Deaf students because she didn't understand Deaf culture and I had to interpret it anyway.

When Good Things Turn Bad

Being an interpreter was not the only way in which I hid behind other people's opinions. Once my dad finally accepted Jesus, he began to grow in the Lord and was a student of the Bible. He learned fast, and God's wisdom and love began to show up in miraculous ways in his life. I often think of those first few years of his walk with Jesus as making up for the years that were lost to alcohol. It was beautiful and inspiring to watch Jesus come alive in him. I had a front row seat to the way God does miracles in people.

For all the change that happened in my dad, the change was slower for me. Sometimes I struggled when it came to having faith, but I didn't have a compartment for that. I glazed over verses that didn't make sense and highlighted the ones that felt good. For me, God didn't seem big enough to handle contradictions, either the ones I saw in the world or the ones I felt in my heart.

One reason I went to Bible college was because I lacked confidence in my faith. I believed that if I could just go someplace to learn things about the Bible, I would be equipped with the answers I needed to explain to people how to have faith in God. And if I could convince enough people to believe in him, then that would prove I was right and God was true.

I am so thankful for my experience there, but I left Bible college with more questions than answers. And I worried that questions or doubts were somehow wrong, so I didn't voice them or admit my fears. As a result, I wasn't willing to learn anything new about God. I left college still planted in basically the same place I'd left high school—on the sidelines.

The Voice of the Bystander

It happens a lot around sophomore year. You've been a good girl, your friends are good girls, and your parents like it that way. By the time you turn sixteen, you've lived a lot of your life being good and you're not really sure why. And then it happens. Your best friend stops telling you things and starts avoiding you. You hear in the hallways near the water fountain that she was at that party last weekend and she made herself look like a fool by getting drunk. You can't believe it, but you do believe it. When you ask her about it, she calls you Goody Two-Shoes and walks away.

A rebel voice begins to speak, starts to whisper things like, *You think you're better than everyone else. Live a little! Loosen up! Have some fun!* If you are used to living life on the sidelines, it could be nice to get a little attention. You are faced with a choice, and the choice isn't easy. It's deeper than just peer pressure.

The first time I can remember being tempted to have a bystander faith was freshman year. Carrie and I were all BFF-y, and then in the middle of ninth grade we made plans to go to the beach that summer. But by the end of the year, Carrie had made herself some very good friends who weren't me. So she called to talk me out of going to the beach with them.

She tried to make it sound like she wanted to do what was best for me, the classic "it's not you, it's me" excuse. She said she didn't think I would have any fun with them. When I refused to agree with her and insisted that I really wanted to go, she was forced to blurt out the thing that would come to be what I loved and hated about this passion of mine: "We don't want to sit in the hotel room and read the Bible all day."

That is what she said. I was shocked. And mortified. It was then I knew that the worst possible thing they could think, they thought. They saw me as the Jesus Girl. Could it be any worse? *No*, I thought. *No, it could not be. There goes Jesus, messing up my social life.*

I was faced with a choice: trust in Carrie or trust in Jesus. I wanted to trust in Carrie. I wanted to go to the beach with them, but more than that, I wanted them to *want* me to go to the beach with them. It hurt to know they didn't want me there, and it made me mad knowing why.

The Bystander tempts us to stay quiet when it comes to our faith. The Bystander whispered to me that day in my room, *Why do you have to be so serious about God? If you stayed on the sidelines more, people wouldn't have to know what you believe. You go to church, and you stay out of trouble. Let that be enough.*

The Hiding—Listening to the Voice of the Bystander

The voice of the Bystander is a tricky one to identify, mainly because she speaks so subtly, so quietly, and so logically. Listening to this voice might not lead you to do anything wrong, but it just might lead you to not do anything at all.

The main goal of the Bystander is to stay safe, to hang back, to avoid taking a risk. It feels risky to have faith. As uncomfortable as the questions can be, it may feel safer to have them. Because as long as I have questions, I do not have to take any action that requires faith. As long as I doubt God, I don't have to trust him. It can be a tricky little game we play in our minds, a game designed to keep us a safe distance from hurt, disappointment, and failure. We don't want to get close; we simply want to be left alone. At least, that's what we tell ourselves.

The Bible is filled with people who had to get close in order to be healed. In Mark 5:21, we read that Jesus was surrounded by crowds of commoners wanting to see this God-man in action. A man named Jairus pushed his way through the crowd toward Jesus, desperate for a miracle.

When he finally reached Jesus, he fell down at his feet, pleading, "My little daughter is at the point of death; please come and lay your hands on her, that she may get well and live" (Mark 5:23). Jairus wasn't just any man; he was a synagogue official, a very important, respected person. But that day in front of Jesus, he was also a frantic, worried daddy.

Now remember, there was a huge crowd. It was loud, chaotic, and disorganized. People were pressing in to see Jesus, wondering, *What's wrong with Jairus's daughter? Will she die? What is this Jesus going to do?* And just when it seems the story has a plot rising to action with this young, dying girl as the primary character, a bleeding woman shows up on the scene.

Culturally in those days, a woman who was bleeding was considered unclean. Anyone who touched her was also considered unclean, so nobody touched her. That's sad enough, to be shunned because of something you can't help. But even more sad, this woman had been bleeding for twelve long years, and she had spent all her money to find a doctor who could help her. There wasn't one to be found, and her condition grew worse.

The woman lived her life as a bystander. When Jesus came to town, she went out with everyone else to watch him pass by, but she stayed a safe distance from everyone, knowing she was unwelcome in society. She heard about Jesus, and she knew in her heart, *This man is my only chance.* So she moved toward him, risking public humiliation, shame, and rejection. It would have been easier for her to remain hidden as she had done for the past twelve years. But her need for healing outweighed her desire to hide.

That is often the case for us as well. We can live on the sidelines, comfortable to accept our parents' faith as true and move through life without risking much. But then something happens—we move out of the house, we have a fight with a friend, we get our heart broken—and suddenly, the sidelines don't seem so safe anymore. A bystander faith isn't enough. We have to step out from the crowd and find out, *Is this Jesus really strong enough, big enough . . . enough?*

The bleeding woman was about to find out. She didn't want to be a bother; she only wanted to be well. This man Jesus was her last hope. In an attempt to remain safely hidden among the crowd, she approached Jesus from behind and touched his cloak, knowing that would be enough to make her well. She had great faith but little self-esteem. She felt both desperate and invisible.

> Immediately the flow of her blood was dried up; and she felt in her body that she was healed of her affliction. Immediately Jesus, perceiving in Himself that the power proceeding from Him had gone forth, turned around in the crowd and said, "Who touched My garments?" (Mark 5:29–30)

She didn't speak up right away. In fact, she waited long enough for the disciples to roll their eyes at Jesus and point out the huge crowd of people all around. Of course people were touching him! Everyone was touching everyone. How could he expect to identify one solitary touch? But Jesus continued looking around for her.

That must have been when she realized she had to identify herself. As much as she wanted to go unnoticed, her days of having a bystander faith were over. "But the woman fearing and trembling, aware of what had happened to her, came and fell down before Him and told Him the whole truth" (Mark 5:33). No more hiding in the crowd. No more trying to sneak healing from a distance. It was time for her to be seen. So she told him the whole truth. She stepped out from behind her comfort zone and fell at the feet of Jesus.

His response to her was both loving and life-giving. Just when it seems as though Jesus should be hurrying to reach the sick daughter of the synagogue official rather than wasting time talking with a woman who is rejected and outcast, he does something completely unexpected. The young girl wasn't the only daughter who needed his touch; he called this bleeding woman *daughter* as well: "Daughter, your faith has made you well; go in peace and be healed of your affliction" (Mark 5:34). Consider how that word must have warmed her heart after so many years on the sidelines. Can you imagine the day she had after that truth encounter with Jesus?

Meanwhile, Jairus, the very important synagogue official, was still waiting for Jesus to follow him to his house and heal his daughter. But word quickly traveled that they were too late; his young daughter had died. I can't help but wonder if the bleeding woman stayed around long enough to hear about the girl. Even though Jesus knew this little girl was close to death, he still took the time to find the woman who touched his garments, to see her, to speak to her, and to make her whole.

His timing and lack of panic even in the middle of great need amazes me, as does his ability to see and know and love without boundaries. He told Jairus not to be afraid but to believe. And there is that word again: *believe*. The crowd was watching to see what Jesus would *do*. Jairus was urging Jesus to *do*. Jesus tells him to *believe*.

When they arrived at Jairus's house, Jesus approached the bed where the girl lay motionless. He took the girl by the hand and simply said to her, "Get up!" And she did.

Both of these girls were so dearly loved by Jesus. But for them to be healed, there had to be a touch. And touch requires closeness. Hiding behind a comfort zone of supposed safety is not an option. Being good while on the sidelines offers a false sense of safety at best. It is only when we begin to listen and believe the voice of Jesus that we will understand he alone is our safe place. Just like the sick woman and the little girl, he calls us daughters as well.

I don't believe Jesus asks us to step away from the sidelines just to prove that we are willing to. He doesn't need our grand gestures or platform speeches. The only action he asks of the bystander is simply that she move toward him, just like the woman in the crowd. It was a simple act of faith, and it was the only one required. Simply move toward Jesus and he will take care of the rest.

The Finding—On Hearing God's Voice

Chloe's mom had been gone for months. She and her dad were trying to navigate life without her, but it wasn't going so well. They fought a lot, and she sometimes thought it may have actually been easier if her mom had died. Chloe felt guilty for feeling that way, but it was true. The rejection of knowing her mom left on purpose was becoming too much to bear.

One night after fighting with her dad, she thought about her neighbor, Melanie, a sweet woman with sons who had recently left home for college. Melanie was kind, loved God, and seemed to take a special liking to Chloe. She thought about walking next door just to be around a mother, even if it wasn't her own.

An hour earlier, Melanie was pushing her cart through the grocery store aisle, thinking, *Baking soda . . . baking soda. I haven't made cookies from scratch in years. Maybe ever?* Her college-age son had only one request from his mom—homemade chocolate chip cookies. It was strange to Melanie—she always used the ready-made dough. Just the same, she went to the store to gather the last of her ingredients. The date on her baking soda was long past expired, and she needed to replace it. When she arrived home, it was already dark, and she began to set out all the items she would need: the mixer, sugar, eggs, butter, flour, baking soda. Just as she lined everything up on the counter, the doorbell rang.

Meanwhile, Chloe stood on the porch steps. *This is stupid*, she thought. *What am I even doing here?* She turned to leave just as the porch lamp came on and the warm light exposed her standing there. Melanie opened the door, clearly surprised to see her, but not in a bad way. "Hi, Chloe! How are you?"

Chloe looked at her feet and considered telling Melanie she just wanted to say hi and then run right home. But the idea of going back to her lonely house and her upset dad compelled her to say instead, "Um, I'm okay. Are you . . . ? Well, could I . . . ?" Chloe felt stupid and awkward. How do you say, *I just want to be around you because you are nice and kind of like a mother and would that be okay?*

A thought came to her. "Do you wanna, like, make cookies or something?"

Melanie paused and stood staring at Chloe, shocked. Then her face lit up. "You're never going to believe this . . ."

As Chloe followed her through the house, she briefly wondered what the deal was. *Why is Melanie acting so weird?* At that moment, they entered the kitchen and she saw the ingredients spread out on the counter, ready to be made into cookies. Chloe looked at Melanie, confused. "But how did you know?"

Melanie laughed a beautiful, angel-like laugh. "Chloe, don't you see? God knew you were coming! He did this just for you."

When my friend Melanie told me this story, it brought tears to my eyes. Chloe was a young girl who had lived most of her life in the shelter of her parents' home. But when her mom left, her safe place was no longer so safe. She needed to find a new one. After the fight with her dad, she could have done a number of things to make herself feel better. She chose Melanie's warm, loving home. It was a small step of faith, but it had a big payoff. She arrived on Melanie's doorstep wondering if she would feel overlooked forever. She left with a simple picture of God's love for her that she would not soon forget.

A New Kind of Hiding

There is a Hebrew name for God that is especially sweet to me. It is *El Roi*, and it means "the God who sees me." Growing up a good girl on the sidelines, I have often doubted that God sees me. Chloe doubted that too.

Sideline living felt safe. And living out my parents' faith wasn't a bad thing, but at some point it had to become mine. Because what if your heart breaks? You are the one who feels the pain. What if you are faced with hard choices? You are the one who has to live with the discomfort of saying no. What if your parents' faith falters? You are the one who has to decide if yours will too. There is only one safe place, and the sidelines isn't it.

In John 4, a Samaritan woman stood at a well and listened as a Jewish man told her everything she had ever done. As she listened to him talk about her life, she tried to change the subject, but it didn't work exactly. He wanted to talk about her heart while she was trying to talk about church.

"Our fathers worshiped in this mountain," she said, "and you people say that in Jerusalem is the place where men ought to worship" (John 4:20).

The man answered her question and then brought the conversation straight back to where they began, like a truth boomerang. "God is spirit, and those who worship Him must worship in spirit and truth" (John 4:24). Not on a mountain or in Jerusalem. Not in shadows or in half-heartedness. Not from the sidelines or as a spectator.

In spirit and in truth.

As they continued talking, the woman realized that this was no mere man but the Messiah. And when she saw this truth, she ran from him and told everyone in the city, "Come, see a man who told me all the things that I have done; this is not the Christ, is it?" (John 4:29). Because of her story, many from the city believed in Jesus. But as more and more began to believe, read what they said to the woman:

> It is no longer because of what you said that we believe, *for we have heard for ourselves* and know that this One is indeed the Savior of the world. (John 4:42, emphasis added)

Have you heard for yourself? That is the question every believer must answer. We have to decide if we believe because of what someone else said or because we've heard it for ourselves.

Think of your favorite books and movies. Nearly all of them tell the story of a bystander who is faced with a tragedy they need to recover from, an insult they need to avenge, a mystery they need to solve, an obstacle they need to overcome. And none of that can be done from the sidelines. Our characters are faced with a choice, a moment in time where they have to decide if they will step out in faith or remain where they are.

Frodo had to leave the Shire in order to destroy the ring.

Allie had to leave behind society (as well as her mother's expectations) in order to find Noah and true love.

Neo had to choose between staying in the Matrix or seeing what was really true.

Katniss had to leave District 12 and compete in the hunger games in order to save the life of her sister.

Harry had to leave Hogwarts and venture out on a quest to destroy evil once and for all.

Jesus calls you out from sideline living to experience life with him. This doesn't mean if you are naturally introverted that you have to become loud and outgoing to live out your faith. He doesn't ask you to change your personality or to become someone you aren't. He invites you instead to embrace the you he made you to be, whether you are quiet, thoughtful, friendly, excitable, giggly, curious, or a mix of them all. He simply asks you to come to him as yourself, willing and open and ready to receive whatever he has to offer.

This kind of movement toward Jesus paints the picture of a life motivated by love rather than by fear. Don't let fear push you around. Instead, be open to the leading of Love.

Truths to Remember When the Bystander Begins to Speak

God sees you. Not because of what you have done or not done but because you are loved. "O LORD, You have searched me and known me. You know when I sit down and when I rise up; You understand my thought from afar" (Ps. 139:1–2).

You have to hear for yourself. It is good to trust your parents' faith, but it has to become your own. "It is no longer because of what you said that we believe, *for we have heard for ourselves* and know that this One is indeed the Savior of the world" (John 4:42, emphasis added).

Trusting God is not stepping into darkness. Faith simply means stepping off the sidelines straight into love. "Daughter, your faith has made you well" (Mark 5:34).

the judge

Hiding behind Her Rules

For you are not under law but under grace.

—*Romans 6:14*

It was a hard day of first grade. No sooner did we arrive home from school than I realized I had left my lunch box in the coat closet of my classroom. Which meant my banana peel was officially beginning to stink it all up. Which also meant I would have to take my lunch in a brown bag tomorrow. Which also meant people would notice that I had forgotten my lunch box in the coat closet. Which also meant that I would have to stoop down and rummage through fallen coats while looking for my lunch box tomorrow. Which somehow, in my six-year-old mind, seemed to mean that I was a bad person because I made a mistake.

I know it all sounds ridiculous. I want to shout to my kid-self, "Lighten up!" But even small failures were devastating to me as early as first grade. My mom finally convinced my friend Audra to find my lunch box for me the next day at school. I watched nervously from my desk as she bounded over to the coat closet to search for it, her scrawny legs folded up beneath her as she bent down to find what belonged to me. Such freedom she had! It was a great relief not to have to do that myself. People wouldn't have to know I forgot my lunch box. People wouldn't have to know I made a mistake.

For those of us who live life by the rules, we often fear the judgment of others, but our worst judge is ourselves.

When Good Things Turn Bad

My senior year of high school, all the seniors in our youth group received a book from our youth pastor. Each chapter described a different spiritual discipline for the Christian life: prayer, Bible reading, journaling, evangelism, etc. By the time I headed off to my first year of Bible college, I had that book marked up in the best way. I had been a believer for ten years by now, so I thought I knew what it took to live the Christian life right. This book supported my bullet-point Jesus, and I was confidently on my way to becoming who I thought God wanted me to be.

Things like reading your Bible, prayer, journaling—these things are good and beautiful. The problem is not the fact that we do them; it is our good girl interpretation of what it means when we do them. And for those of us who never do these things at all, there can be a great sense of shame that washes over us for not being a good enough Christian. I have lived as a believer *in* God, but I do not always live *from* God. In high school, I was a child of the God of grace, but I was looking for life in the law.

I would try hard to muster up the motivation I thought was required of me to be a good Christian, but there was always a sense of desperation, frustration, and fear that perhaps I wasn't doing enough. That was the problem with my checklist Christianity: sometimes my list remained unchecked.

I tried to win in my walk with God, but secretly I always expected defeat. If I prayed for ten minutes, I knew I could have prayed for twenty. If I read one chapter of Psalms, I wondered if I should have read two. I can't count how many New Year's Days I resolved to read through the entire Bible in a year because I was trying to satisfy the law I had in my head.

Occasionally, I was able to live up to the rules I thought God wanted me to follow. Then I would look down my nose at those who didn't or couldn't. But only a week later I would find myself in their same condition, unable to perform anymore, defeated from all the effort. Instead of facing the failure and allowing the law to show me my need for a Savior, I consoled my failure with new and improved intentions to prove myself by myself. And the cycle continued.

The Voice of the Judge

Some people don't like rules. They see rules as the enemy, like a prison guard with a whip and handcuffs. As a good girl, I saw rules as more of a fickle friend. When I followed them and was able to keep them well, rules treated me right. They gave me a measuring stick to let me know how I was doing. But those times when I couldn't measure up or I bent under the weight of them, those rules turned on me fast. They became burdensome and judgmental—a heavy, unwelcome enemy. I could never quite figure out how to make them like me *all* the time.

Still, I like knowing the rules. If the sign says Don't Touch, I don't touch. If it says Keep Out, I stay away. If the form is due on Friday, I'll turn it in on Thursday just in case. If the doctor says take one in the morning and one at night, I am sure to space them out exactly twelve hours. And even though I admit to occasionally bringing candy into the movie theater, I am always worried that the ticket person will search my bags and throw me out for smuggling in a bottle of water and two peppermint patties.

If the rules are ambiguous or unknown, it's worse. I worry if there is no meter when I park on the street downtown. *Am I allowed to park here? Will I get a ticket?*

So you can imagine what happens when I break the rules, even when I don't mean to. When you are a good girl who finds her identity in her performance, mistakes mean punishment, even when it is an accident.

One sunny day during my junior year of college, I was on my way to the mall to use a 20 percent off coupon. I was listening to Peter Gabriel sing "In Your Eyes," the windows were down, my heart was alive with the hope that comes in springtime. With my left foot propped up on my seat, I casually turned into the mall parking lot. I didn't see the car coming.

Even though the girl driving the other car got a ticket for driving too fast, the accident was my fault. An hour later, after riding in the ambulance with her (she had a broken leg, by the way—oh the guilt!), I was sitting on a gurney in the hall of the hospital. I remember looking up at the police officer and asking him if I was going to jail. Because in my mind, people who cause car accidents are criminals and should be punished. And now I was one.

I will never forget the look of surprise and amusement on that police officer's face as he assured me I would not be going to jail. I will also never forget the relief I felt.

In other parts of life where there are no rules at all, I become irritated and slightly irrational. Like in art class my sophomore year when my teacher didn't give us any instruction for our work that day, saying instead that we were free to express ourselves on paper in whatever way came natural for us. I was a wreck. *What am I supposed to do here?!* Creativity doesn't come with a rule book, but it seemed to me that Christianity did.

The Hiding—Listening to the Voice of the Judge

It's hard sometimes to tell the difference between the voice of the Judge and the voice of God, mainly because sometimes the voice of the Judge sounds a lot like some of the things we hear in church. Listen again. The Judge speaks with an air of importance and strictness, while God issues an invitation in gentleness and love.

The Judge uses *never* and *always* a lot in her vocabulary. She makes up rules for things that wouldn't normally have rules—things like *I'll always remember my friends' birthdays and get them a present.* The Judge who finds her safe place in her rules focuses on the rule rather than the heart. Forgetting a birthday becomes all about her rather than about her friend. *Stupid me! I can't believe I did that!*

The only reason we know to make up rules for ourselves is because we have grown up in a rules environment. And that isn't a bad thing, unless the church is reduced to a place where we are to follow a list of dos and do-nots. I suppose it began with the Ten Commandments. Do you know what they are? I don't. I mean, not off the top of my head anyway. But God gave Moses the Ten Commandments to give to the people, along with a long list of other rules and regulations they were to carefully keep. At first they were super excited, saying, "Everything you have said we will do!" But it didn't take them long to realize those rules were impossible, heavy, and nothing but a burden.

So why did God give a list of impossible rules anyway? Do you really think he expected his people to be able to follow them all perfectly? Let's think about it. One of the Ten Commandments is this: do not covet your neighbor's house, meaning don't want what you can't have. Seriously? I want what I can't have at least once an hour. I want my hair to lose the frizz. I want chocolate for dinner. I want a smaller big toe. I want the size of my nose to be a little more proportional to the size of my face. I want her talent. I want their money. I want his fame. I want what I can't have. But you know the answer to being free from wanting what you can't have? It isn't someone telling you to stop.

The Bible says in 1 Corinthians 15:56, "The power of sin is the law." That means if I tell you not to think about pigs, it's going to be difficult for you not to think about pigs. That's because the power of sin is the law. In other words, the surest way to get someone to do something is to tell them not to do it.

It's like when my mom told my sister and I we weren't allowed to go under the bridge. The truth is, if she never told us not to, we probably wouldn't have been so curious about it. But knowing it was forbidden made it that much more appealing. *What happens under there? What are we missing out on by avoiding it?*

The purpose of the law is to call our attention to the fact that we can't keep it. And once we realize that, the law leads us to the only One who can.

If we focus on the law, we only see the law. If we are constantly trying not to do something, chances are it will become difficult, if not impossible, not to do it because it becomes our focus.

Don't talk back to your mom.

Don't give in to peer pressure.

Don't cuss.

Don't be judgmental.

Don't make out with your boyfriend.

Don't go to that party.

Don't listen to certain music.

Don't gossip.

It's exhausting. Especially for good girls because we tend to be able to avoid a lot of the "big sins," the ones that are obvious and external. But quiet, private sins trip us up. The Judge keeps our focus on the dos and the do-nots.

We need a new focus.

The Finding—On Hearing God's Voice

Jesus came so we could stop looking at the law, thinking about the law, and trying to keep the law. Jesus came so we could look at him instead. "Therefore the Law has become our tutor to lead us to Christ, so that we may be justified by faith" (Gal. 3:24). I've heard pastors compare the law to a mirror. If I have dirt on my face, I go to the mirror, and it shows me the truth. The mirror isn't bad; it simply reveals what is there. At the same time, the mirror by itself has no power to clean my face. I would be a crazy person if I took the mirror from the wall and rubbed my face with it, trying to clean off the dirt. But that is what good girls do with the law. We believe that as Christians, it's our job to keep it.

Only Jesus could keep God's rules perfectly. You don't have to understand all the Ten Commandments or the hundreds of laws listed in the Bible, though learning about them will show you even more your great need for God. You simply have to know Jesus came—not to destroy the law but to fulfill it so that we no longer have to.

That doesn't mean now we are to break the rules whenever we want. Of course not. Instead, it means keeping the rules is not the way to find favor with God.

We have an enemy who would do anything to keep us distracted from Jesus. If tempting us to break the rules doesn't work, then he'll do the opposite: tempt us to keep them for all the wrong reasons. The voice of the Judge wants us to keep living by the rules rather than living by faith. Following the rules gives us some feeling of control, some sense of order and safety. When we look to rules rather than Jesus as our safe place, that's when we become rigid, judgmental, and ultimately un-free.

That voice also tries to convince us to measure the success or failure of others by the bad things they do and the good things they fail to do. We carry around our good girl measuring sticks, pointing out all the ways we are better because we can handle the rules

But if you are anything like me, you know there are two sides to this rule thing. On the one hand, I feel good about myself when I'm able to keep the rules. I feel right and better in a way. I can look at the girls who break the rules and shake my head in pity, believing I'm better off. The rules are my friend.

Then I mess up, and one of two things happens. Either I feel horrible about myself, telling myself things like, *I should have known better. I'm such a loser. I'm such a bad Christian.* Or I blow it off, thinking, *Well, I know I messed up, but nobody's perfect. And at least I'm not doing what those other girls are doing.*

A life of listening to the Judge forces us down the road of self-importance ("Look how great I am because I follow the rules"), self-hatred ("Look how awful I am because I messed up"), or self-complacency ("I messed up, but look at how bad everyone else is compared to me"). What do all these roads have in common?

Self.

Jesus shows up on the scene and calls us out of ourselves. He stands at the intersection of all those self-roads and reminds us that there is a better way to live. It's not by hiding behind rules but by dwelling in relationship with him. There is no road map to living this kind of life. In fact, there may not be any road at all. When we choose the way of Jesus, it's as if the road of rules disappears below us, and we are lifted up and out of the bullet-point life and into a world of adventure.

When you focus on the law, you may be able to obey the rules, but you don't experience much life. You may still feel left out, alone, deprived of fun. It doesn't feel fair. Or you may huddle together with other good Christians and form your proud little group of goodness. When we only focus on obedience, we lose the heart behind it.

Jesus didn't come to earth so we would obey the law. He came to fulfill the law so we don't have to look at it anymore. Obedience is still important, but now it comes from a different place. Jesus invites us to a new and better way. He does ask for our obedience, but it is no longer obedience to the law. Now we are called as believers to be obedient *to the truth* (see Gal. 5:7).

I know you're probably wondering what I could possibly mean by that, wondering what the difference is between being obedient to the law and obedient to the truth.

What does that even look like?

A New Kind of Hiding

Obedience to the truth means when I go to that party where they're doing all the stuff I'm not supposed to do, I can choose not to do it and I don't feel *deprived*; I feel *free*. It means when my parents give me a curfew that is earlier than my girlfriends', I can come home on time and not fight it; I can be joyful rather than grumpy. It doesn't mean I will always feel joyful, but at least I have that choice. It means when my best friend makes choices that are seven shades of crazy, I can pray for her and ask God for wisdom and compassion rather than judge her and talk about her behind her back. I can do all of these things not because I am so strong and great, but because Jesus is. And he is the Truth. And he lives in me.

It means when I am tempted to reduce my walk with Jesus down to a list, I can remember these questions: Is a life of dos and do-nots what Jesus came into this world for? Is this the kind of experience that men and women throughout history have given their lives for, so that we simply follow the rules? Are those rules and regulations worth dying for? *Dying?!*

No, they aren't worth dying for. *People* are worth dying for. Not so they will follow a set of rules, but so they will live a full, abundant, free, graceful life.

God's Word says this: "The only thing that counts is faith expressing itself through love" (Gal. 5:6 NIV). Paul wrote that to the church in Galatia, a group of believers who were listening to the voice of the Judge in a major way. They were beginning to believe things about God that were contrary to what they had been taught. They were trying to live by the rules rather than by faith. Paul wrote them a passionate letter to remind them what it's all about, to remind them what matters. And what matters isn't a list of rules but faith expressing itself through love.

More than any other good girl voice, the Judge is probably the main one that urges you to find answers to the question *What am I supposed to do?*

Figure it out.

Follow the rules.

Check off the list.

And by all means, *get it right.*

God does not want us to find our safe place in a list of rules. When I imagine a new and different place to hide, I think of a small boy standing in the midst of a large, hungry crowd by the seashore so many years ago. I think of thousands of men and women and other boys just like him. I think of his dark hair blowing in the sea breeze, of him holding his lunch close, of bread and fish wrapped in a cloth at the bottom of the basket his mother packed that morning. A man appears beside him and calls out loudly over his head, "Here is a boy with five small barley loaves and two small fish, but how far will they go among so many?" The boy looks up into the man's eyes. He looks flustered, tired, doubtful.

But from a distance, the Teacher is visible. He is different from the other grown-ups. He seems to have something they don't have. Hope? A plan? A secret? He smiles and gives directions for the people to sit.

Waves of people begin to still on the mountainside near the sea. They are sitting in groups of fifty and one hundred, because the Teacher had directed them to do so. The boy sits too—waiting. He watches the Teacher take his mama's bread, give thanks, and they eat. Impossibly, the thousands eat. There is laughter and fullness all around. The boy chews and swallows and can't believe it, but it's true. He wonders about this miracle man, and he smiles on the inside, eager to get home and tell his mama that the man told her morning bread to multiply—*and it obeyed.*

Then I think of the men in the boat later that same night, these friends of Jesus, these followers, these chosen believers. They got in their boat in the dark without the Teacher. Three miles out the waters began to rage rough, and they rowed frantically, fearing for their lives. Their Teacher impossibly walked toward them on the water alone, and their worry rose to panic, because *how?* But they heard his voice, they let him in, and their boat immediately reached land.

The same crowd from lunch followed them, meeting Jesus at the shore and asking the questions of sight and logic and earthly things. *How did you get here? You didn't take a boat. What did you do, walk on the water?*

He tells them they only followed him because their stomachs were filled with the loaves and fishes, and now they are hungry again. He tells them about working for food that endures to eternal life, the kind the Son of Man alone can give.

Then they ask the question of every good girl, of every person who wants to be pleasing and to do well and to live right. *What must we do to do the works God requires?*

What must we do? Tell us what to do. We'll do anything. Anything. Where is my list? Where is the measuring stick? What are the rules? I'll do them, if only I knew what they were! And so Jesus, the Teacher, the Lover, the Savior of the whole world tells them: "This is the work of God, that you believe in Him whom He has sent" (John 6:29).

A boy in a crowd with a small lunch. Friends in a boat with a lot of fear. A crowd looking for a list. The answer is the same for all of them, as it is for us: *the work of God is to believe in the One he has sent.*

Does that feel risky? Too easy? Too hard? Too invisible? Believing our lives are hidden in Christ can be a messy process, one filled with questions and doubt, sacrifice and struggle. But when we hold on to Jesus and know he is God, when we believe in him as sure as oxygen and gravity, when we trust him when he says that the only work he asks of us is the work of belief, he will not disappoint. The voice of the Judge keeps us in hiding, looking at the law, trying desperately to live up to the law, and holding others up to it too. The voice of God offers us freedom, looking only to Jesus.

Receive him, friend. Not just for your salvation but for this moment. Breathe in the sweetness of acceptance. Release the gavel that hovers in your mind, the one ready to fall and declare you responsible to pay for your own sin, the one you pound on the table, demanding that others pay for theirs as well. It is not for you to judge, it is not for you to punish. It is simply not. For. You. Because really, if we do not receive and extend to ourselves and others the abundance of grace and patience and love that is given for free from the only One who can give it, then how can we really live?

Truths to Remember When the Judge Begins to Speak

The work of God is to believe. You are asked to simply trust. "This is the work of God, that you believe in Him whom He has sent" (John 6:29).

Only faith can make it right. "Therefore the Law has become our tutor to lead us to Christ, so that we may be justified by faith" (Gal. 3:24).

We live by grace alone. Grace plus anything is no longer grace. "You are not under law but under grace" (Rom. 6:14).

the intellectual

Hiding behind Her Report Card

Make a little room in your plans for romance again,
Anne, girl. All the degrees and scholarships in
the world can't make up for the lack of it.

—Aunt Josephine to Anne Shirley in Anne of Green Gables

Shauna was a good girl who came fairly consistently to youth group several years ago. She never said much when we were all together, so it took me several years to get to know her. One thing I learned about her early on: Shauna took school very seriously. She never missed a day of high school. When our youth group went on a weekend retreat that required students to miss a half day, Shauna didn't go. When she didn't feel well, she pushed through it. When her family went on vacation, they rigidly worked around her school schedule.

Shauna worried about school, about tests, about homework and projects and finishing things on time. She was concerned about her grades, about getting into college, about being outdone by other students.

I sat in the bleachers that hot day in late May when Shauna graduated at the top of her class and received the perfect attendance award. I respected her for taking her schooling seriously. I was proud of the work she had done. But I imagined Shauna five years from that day, walking into her first job interview. They won't ask about her GPA in high school. They won't request a copy of her perfect attendance award. Yet so many hours of energy were spent with concern over those things. Not just concern, but near *obsession*. As I sat there staring out at the sea of graduates sweating through their black robes, I thought of all she sacrificed to have perfect attendance, and I couldn't help but wonder if it was worth it.

When Good Turns Bad

According to my six-year-old, the definition of a mean person is anyone who disagrees with her. If she isn't right, then she is not okay, and you are mean. It sounds funny to say it like that, but I can relate in a way.

Shauna was obsessed with being right, being the best, being on top. We are taught early that being right is best and being wrong means you get red marks on your paper. I don't like red marks on my paper. And red marks come in many different forms. It could be rejection from your first choice of colleges, correction from a friend when you pronounce a word wrong, a disapproving look from a parent when your report card is less than your best, being scolded by your coach when you're late for practice. Red marks show up in the mirror when we look into it and see a girl who isn't measuring up.

My junior year of college I transferred from a small Bible college to a large university in North Carolina. My grades weren't super at Bible college, and I was eager for a redo. I went from living in a dorm with girls to living at home with my parents. I went from a major that I wasn't super passionate about to one that had me excited to wake up and go to class. I distinctly remember making a decision at the beginning of my junior year: *I'm going to focus on school at the expense of everything else. I don't really need people that much anyway.*

My parents and I spent lots of time and money on my education, so to focus on my schoolwork was wise. I finished at the top of my class, standing with a choice few at graduation. It was a proud day and rightly so. But in many ways it was a lonely day, because for all the hours I spent studying, I spent precious few cultivating close relationships with people. As a new student in a new school and a new town, developing relationships was risky, but developing my knowledge was safe and predictable. So that's what I did, at the expense of most everything else. I was able to avoid the academic red marks, but I ignored the needs I had in other areas.

It isn't bad to care about grades. Of course not! But when *care* morphs into *obsession*, that report card can become a dangerous hiding place we run to in order to find importance. The voice of the Intellectual then becomes the ruling voice in our lives, drowning out the voice of God.

The Voice of the Intellectual

I didn't always do my homework right when I got home from school. But I always did my homework. Granted, it may have been in the ridiculously late hours of the night, but I can't remember a time when I simply chose not to do it on purpose without a very good reason.

Once my mom tried to talk me out of turning something in on time. Yes, you read that right. You know you're a good girl when your mother tries to convince you not to care so much about your homework. I probably procrastinated dangerously close to a deadline and the stress was most likely reaching nuclear levels. She begged me to simply go to bed, turn my homework in late, and take whatever penalty would come my way.

From my horrified reaction, you would have thought she had suggested I cut off my right arm. I couldn't believe she would actually suggest I turn my homework in late. *Seriously?! Does she even know what that would mean?*

Looking back, I'm not sure I knew what that would mean. I colored it eleven shades of horrible in my mind, but the truth is, it probably wouldn't have been that big of a deal.

Some people need parents looking over their shoulder to make sure they do their work. But people like you and me? We need someone to tell us to take a break.

Taking a break doesn't feel like an option for the Intellectual, mainly because she knows all those other smart, dedicated people are not taking breaks. They are forging ahead, joining clubs, attending study groups, preparing for the SAT, making color-coded index cards, getting ahead of us in class rank.

The voice of the Intellectual tries to convince us that breaks are for the weak, and that we will never be the best unless we work ourselves tirelessly. Stress is the norm. A busy schedule means we're accomplishing things. All-nighters are our rite of passage. And so we are left feeling like we are always behind, trying to catch up. The problem is, we aren't sure what exactly we're chasing.

The Hiding—When We Listen to the Voice of the Intellectual

When I first met Lucy, I subconsciously labeled her as just like me only better. We had a lot in common. We both loved *Real Simple* magazine, we both worked with the youth group, and we even liked the same television shows. But she seemed more put together than

I was. She didn't just read *Real Simple*; she cut out articles and organized them into an intricate filing system according to topic. She was such a good girl.

Lucy led a small group and went on every youth trip. She seemed to be the leader all the girls looked up to and wanted to be like. She was such a good Christian.

I liked her immediately and wanted to know her better. But there was something about her that kept me at arm's length. After hearing her story, I now know what it was: Lucy was in hiding.

On the outside, Lucy's childhood home looked like every other. But when she was little and her mom announced she would be having another baby, Lucy's world began to shift. Her father was not happy about the pregnancy. He was angry and said he wished it weren't true. As a young girl, Lucy wondered if her father had felt the same way when she was born.

She began to form an image of herself that day as a girl who was unwanted. An unwelcome voice began to speak lies to her, and she began to believe it: *You are worthless.*

Lucy felt rejected by her father, which led to a false belief that she was worthless and unwanted. But she didn't want anyone to know that she was worthless and unwanted, so she set out to prove her own worth by becoming the best at everything.

She did a fantastic job. She began to listen to another voice, one that sounds a lot like the Actress: *You only have worth because you perform well.*

When Lucy was ten, her mom got sick, and she and her little brother were left in the care of their father, a man who was unfit for the job. So Lucy took care of herself. She made spaghetti, swept floors, and made sure her baby brother was okay. She remembers hearing *Sesame Street* playing in the living room but not having time to sit and watch. There was too much work to do.

Can you even imagine a ten-year-old carrying the weight of her world on her own tiny shoulders? Things were not as they should be. Little girls are to be protected. They should not have to protect themselves.

During this time Lucy began to believe that she could not trust anyone but herself. No one would take care of her. Rather than collapse in despair or self-pity, she chose to listen to and believe the voice of the Heroine: *Be strong and responsible. You have to handle this.* And she did.

She began to believe that the only person she could ever depend on was herself. She did well in school. She got the lead in plays. She was involved in the youth group at church. She excelled in music. She eventually became the valedictorian of her graduating class. And it's as if the Judge and the Intellectual went on a date, conspired a plan, and together whispered to her, *You are better than everyone, because look at what you've survived.*

Lucy believed she had to be the smartest girl in the room. And most of the time she was. Being the smart girl set her apart from others, and she seemed to like it that way. She could control her knowledge; she could not control people. She had figured out how to make life work without anyone else. The only problem in the midst of all that success was that she was not free.

Behind her good grades, responsibility, and good performance, Lucy was a tangled mess. She had red marks all over the paper of her life, and she didn't know what to do with them. The voice of the Intellectual tried telling her to fix it, but she didn't know how.

No one really knew Lucy because Lucy didn't really know herself. The sweet good news of Jesus is that he longs to call us out from behind those places where we are hiding our mess from the world. Lucy was no exception.

I had the amazing privilege of being in a small group with Lucy. We were all grown up and married, and she had successfully kept all of her friends at a long arm's length. While on a beach trip together, we told Lucy we felt we didn't really know her, and we asked if she would be willing to share more of her life story with us.

In the spirit of wanting to be a good friend, Lucy agreed to share. She was guarded at first, but there came a point when she realized she was holding back. That was when the floodgates opened: the selfishness of her father, the abuse they experienced at his hand, the heartache of her mom's sickness, and the responsibility she felt for all of it. Once the tears began, they didn't stop. As she talked, it was as if all those voices she had been listening to were losing their power, one at a time. When she was finished, she sat there feeling empty, wondering who she was without them. She went home broken and exposed.

The Finding—On Hearing God's Voice

In her desperate, needy state, Lucy began to read Psalm 63, and a new voice began to speak: "For You have been my help, and in the shadow of Your wings I sing for joy" (Ps. 63:7). In that moment, the truth winked brightly up at her from the pages of her Bible. Because she was no longer reading through the filter of those good girl voices and had instead opened herself up to the voice of truth, Lucy realized in those words that she didn't have to hide anymore. She didn't have to perform to prove her worth. She didn't have to take care of herself by herself. Though there would be months of healing ahead for her, freedom began to bloom in her that day.

Lucy wasn't to blame for what her dad did. She was just a kid, so she did the only thing she knew to do when she heard those good girl voices speaking: she believed them. She could have chosen to listen to other voices: *Your dad doesn't love you, so find a boy who does.* Or maybe, *Nobody cares about you; you are worthless, so just give up.* But she chose to hide behind her goodness rather than her rebellion. Neither hiding place is safe.

As good girls, we subconsciously label ourselves as the strong ones, the responsible ones, the sweet ones, or the right ones. We try to stand tall and capable as the good Christian who has the answers. Or we begin to doubt our faith when we don't. But Jesus is calling us to a deeper, truer, freer identity. All he wants is simply you—minus your good work, minus your perfect attendance, minus your politeness, minus your right answers, minus your straight A's. When you really believe that, you may discover that all you want is Jesus, simply Jesus. Not just to get to heaven or to help you be a good person or do the right thing or get into college, but to simply love and be loved by him.

A New Kind of Hiding

Being the smartest girl in the room is not a bad thing, it's a beautiful thing. Beautiful, that is, until we have to be the smartest girl in order to be okay with ourselves. If we put our faith in our intellect, we will never be satisfied. Because even if we are the smartest girl in high school, it won't always be that way.

Some of the students in our youth group who graduated a few years ago came back to share with the rising seniors a few things they had learned when they went off to college. Erin was in her second year at a prestigious college, and one thing she said stuck with me: "In high school, I was one of the few really smart students. There were about three or four of us who competed for the top spot in our class. But now that I'm in college, everyone on campus came from a high school where they were one of the top three students in their class. So now I'm just average."

When the Intellectual finds herself in a situation where she is not the smartest and the best, she will feel lost and small. She must find a new place to hide, a true safe place that won't change because of how much she studies or how well she performs on standardized tests. Sometimes in the midst of all our expertise, the concept of humility is completely lost on us. The approval of people and teachers and parents and colleges feels like the most important thing.

What do I mean by humility? William Temple, a teacher and the former Archbishop of Canterbury, once said, "Humility does not mean thinking less of yourself than of other people, nor does it mean having a low opinion of your own gifts. It means freedom from thinking about yourself at all."[1]

The voice of the Intellectual pushes us to think about ourselves above everything and everyone else. In fact, all the other good girl voices do the same thing. They are always encouraging us to look out for ourselves, take care of ourselves, be bigger, better, in control.

Contrast that with 1 Peter 5:6–7, "Therefore humble yourselves under the mighty hand of God, that He may exalt you at the proper time, casting all your anxiety on Him, because He cares for you." I love that these verses talk about humility and anxiety at the same time, because when we don't cast our cares on God, humiliation is often the result. In my mind, humiliation is different from humility.

When we don't humble ourselves before God, we are often humiliated in front of people. And we all know what it is like to feel humiliated.

It's the way your cheeks get red hot when you warmly shake the extended hand of the stranger in Starbucks, only to realize he wasn't reaching in to shake your hand but was offering to plug in your laptop.

It's when the hot guy nods cool in your direction and you wave vigorously back, only to discover the guys' lacrosse team laughing behind you in your blind spot.

It's the pit that sits heavy in your stomach when you accidentally send an "I hate it when she does that!" text to the girl you are talking about rather than the friend you meant to vent to.

It's when your math teacher posts the results of the exam on the wall outside the classroom and everyone can see that you didn't do well.

We feel humiliated in those situations because they are so awkward, so out of our control, so uncomfortable. And also? Because in all those situations we were looking for importance in places other than in God. It's the difference between being brought down low under the mighty, loving hand of God (humility) and being pushed down low under the heavy expectations of ourselves and other people (humiliation).

As we release our right to be right, to know everything, and to look good all the time, we will find a new path of freedom. It's the way of humility, the way of casting all our cares on a loving God, the way of trusting in the Creator of the universe rather than the grade on our paper. When we find ourselves in situations that our intellect cannot get us out of, choosing the way of humility is our best and most life-giving option. That option is only possible as we live our lives hidden with Christ in God. Embracing humility is the opposite of holding on to our rights.

The Actress holds on to her right to be successful.

The Girl Next Door holds on to her right to a good reputation.

The Activist holds on to her right to make a difference.

The Heroine holds on to her right to be responsible.

The Bystander holds on to her right to be left alone.

The Judge holds on to her right to be right.

The Intellectual holds on to her right to have the answers.

The Dreamer holds on to her right to be happy. (We'll talk about her in the next chapter.)

There is great freedom in releasing our right to know everything, to have all the answers. The voice of the Intellectual says, *You have to know everything.* The voice of Jesus whispers, *You just have to know Me.* "Cease striving, and know that I am God" (Ps. 46:10).

When we listen to the voice of the Intellectual, it can affect our ability to have faith in a God we can't see or figure out. Sometimes having faith simply doesn't make sense.

It doesn't make sense that Mary became pregnant without ever having sex.

It doesn't make sense that Jonah lived in the belly of a whale.

It doesn't make sense that Jesus fed over five thousand people with five loaves of bread and a few fish.

Just because *we* haven't figured it out doesn't mean it is impossible. It doesn't make sense to me that an airplane that weighs a literal ton can fly through the sky. But if I wanted to, I could get a book on aerodynamics and study it and soon learn how it does make sense. Flying was impossible . . . until the Wright brothers did it. Walking on the moon was impossible . . . until Neil Armstrong did it. Just because it doesn't make sense *to me* doesn't mean it doesn't make sense *at all*.

Could there be things in the world, in the universe, that don't make sense to *anyone* just like aerodynamics doesn't make sense to me? Could it be possible that the only one to whom a man-swallowing fish and a baby-bearing virgin make sense is God? Am I so arrogant as to believe that the only things that can be true are those things that make sense to *me*?

Sometimes the most intellectual thing we can do is to be at peace with the questions, to say fully and confidently, *I don't know. But I trust God anyway.*

There is a beautiful gift to be found in embracing our smallness, in receiving the gift of knowing from our Father rather than trying to be strong and know everything on our own.

You may be wondering if it's okay to make straight A's. Of course it is. Is it wrong to study hard for tests? Absolutely not. Is it okay if you are the valedictorian of your class? Most definitely. But I think an even more important question to answer is this: *Will you be okay if you aren't?*

Unlike the Intellectual, I do not want to push you toward a

certain school or career or major or grade. I don't want to encourage you to travel the world or cure cancer or become the president. It isn't my job to write your story. That is your job. Well, yours and the God who made you.

I simply want to push you hard into Jesus. Because when we hide in the safety of his presence, when we let go of our impossible expectations to achieve and surpass and outdo, there he stands. He invites you to cast your anxieties on him because he cares for you—grades, college applications, tests, homework, GPA, class rank—all of those things you've been wanting to define you. He will show you the difference between caring about your grades and obsessing over them. He will lead you, step by step, with his mighty hand. Cast all things his way. He is strong, safe, enough.

But you have to know that for yourself. Who do you say he is?

Is he a cartoon?

Is he a stained-glass window?

Is he a hymnal or an overhead screen or a podium?

Is he a has-been or a wannabe or a poser?

Is he ridiculous? Wimpy? Dead?

Or is he a friend? Hero? Servant?

Is he king, brother, and Savior?

Is he enough?

As he was spending time with his disciples, Jesus asked them who people thought he was. "They told Him, saying, 'John the Baptist; others say Elijah; but others, one of the prophets'" (Mark 8:28). People were speculating, guessing who this man was who traveled around and did unpredictable, confusing things like putting mud on the eyes of a blind man. But Jesus didn't try to figure out what everyone else thought of him. Instead, he turned to his disciples—his friends, his followers—and he asked them the most important question, the question that really mattered, the question that would make all the difference: "'But what about you?' he asked. 'Who do you say I am?'" (v. 29 NIV).

Jesus is bigger than you can imagine in your most ridiculous and impossible dreams. And he makes himself small enough to see the most insignificant detail of your day. There is not a hair that falls from your head that he doesn't know about. But it doesn't matter who *I* say he is; it matters who *you* say he is.

As you struggle to answer this question, as you begin to learn what it means to tune out the voice of the Intellectual and tune in to the voice of God, might I invite you to live a different way, a way that circles around one beautiful word?

Grace.

It's all grace, friends. For us, for others, straight from Jesus's heart. And he offers to be our safe place from having to know everything, from needing to always give a right answer, from the cynicism of the world, from the heavy burden of worshiping our report card. Jesus doesn't just walk beside us and help us live life. He gave up his life in order to give his life to us. He came into this world as a baby, upside down just like everyone else. But he set things right side up because he's the only one who could. And his right-side-up spirit lives inside us.

Truths to Remember When the Intellectual Begins to Speak

Nothing exists outside of God. Whether it's a head full of knowledge or a heart longing for relationship, the Bible says all things are held together by God. We do not always have to figure things out. "He is before all things, and in Him all things hold together" (Col. 1:17).

You have the mind of Christ. "Who can know the LORD's thoughts? Who knows enough to teach him? But we understand these things, for we have the mind of Christ" (1 Cor. 2:16 NLT).

You do not have to be the smartest girl in the room. "Therefore humble yourselves under the mighty hand of God, that He may exalt you at the proper time, casting all your anxiety on Him, because He cares for you" (1 Peter 5:6–7).

the dreamer

Hiding behind Her Somedays

> For now we see in a mirror dimly, but then face
> to face; now I know in part, but then I will know
> fully just as I also have been fully known.
>
> —*1 Corinthians 13:12*

I was a junior in high school when I started to think about college. And before I picked a college, I kind of had to know what I wanted to be when I grew up. I changed majors twice, and I had to change colleges when I changed majors. Once I finally graduated, I did what I was trained to do for about six years. And that was it. I'll probably never do it again.

Choosing a major when we are eighteen is crazy. I hear in some other countries it's even earlier. You have to choose a career path before you start high school because the courses you take determine what you'll study in college. And once you choose, you can't really change directions. That means when you're fifteen, you're potentially deciding what you'll be doing when you're fifty.

It was only a few years ago when I finally figured out what I want to do when I grow up. That's pretty normal. So to tell a high school student to stop dreaming of the future is a very unwise thing to do. To be clear, I'm not talking about that kind of dreaming.

When Good Things Turn Bad

When I was sixteen our family decided to leave the church we had attended since I was in sixth grade. I left my familiar youth group and went with my parents all over town to visit churches. And more churches. And then another church. There are a lot of churches in Columbia, South Carolina. So many, in fact, that you could probably visit one a week and not double up in a year.

We finally settled on a small church in a quaint neighborhood near downtown, and I tried to make my way into a new youth group. As a junior, it wasn't easy. Everyone already had their people. I nearly gave up but for one very powerful motivator.

His name was Sam Hunt.

Sam was tall like a basketball player and kind of charming—Jim Halpert from *The Office* charming. A little dorky. Bright eyes. You know. I was sensibly boy crazy at sixteen, so even though I liked boys a lot, I rarely acted on my crushes. I was always attracted to the good boys.

I loved daydreaming about Sam Hunt. I imagined we would go to the same college and drink lattes in a little café near campus. He would write me songs, and I would buy him sweaters. We would take road trips to the beach with friends and eat funnel cakes at the Pavilion and laugh hard late into the night by the bonfire. I wondered what it might be like to stand close to a guy so tall—I knew it would make me feel girly and small and beautiful. I wondered how it might be to have him look deep in my eyes, to have his arm rest casually around my shoulders, to have him call me his girl.

We never went out on a date. We never had a conversation alone that I can remember. It didn't matter. In fact, a date may have ruined it. Because when you actually go on a date, you start to see that the perfect boys aren't all that perfect. And that really does a number on the daydream.

I had a crush, but I'm not sure I actually had a crush on Sam Hunt. He was the face attached to it, but I didn't really know much about him at all. I thought he played basketball, but I think it may have actually been volleyball. No matter. I took what I knew, and I filled in the details to my liking. It was fun. And also ridiculous. When you have a crush on a half-real, half-imaginary boy, you will always be disappointed.

The Voice of the Dreamer

As good girls, our dreams are nearly always nice ones. Fall in love. Have a family. Travel the world. Contribute to a cause. Find a cure for cancer. Dreaming is a lovely thing until we start missing reality because we're hiding in the dream. Until we spend so much time dreaming about traveling the world that we ignore our Spanish homework that might actually help us get there one day. The problem with hiding in your dreams is that you can get stuck inside them. You can hold them too tightly and begin to feel like real life isn't good enough. You miss the living because you are waiting for perfect, and so you let goodness and blessings pass you right on by.

My best friend from high school and I used to play a game we called "Past, Present, Future." We would turn on the radio and the first song that came on represented our past. We would die when Boyz II Men's "It's So Hard to Say Goodbye to Yesterday" came on first because it was just so perfect! It was like a clue that it was time to put the past behind us. Because, you know, that isn't obvious or anything. The second song was always revealing because it represented what was going on in our lives at that moment. We analyzed the lyrics and pulled out meanings to apply to our lives—very scientific and accurate. But the whole point of the game was really getting to that third song, because that one represented our future. We always hoped Vanessa Williams' "Save the Best for Last" would come on as our third song; we took that to mean good things were to come.

It was ridiculous, this game we played. But it proves the point that so much of my time in high school was spent simply trying to figure out my future—where I would live, who I would marry, how many kids I would have, what job I would get, what kind of house we would live in. Again, it isn't bad to dream about our future. But in some ways I think the voice of the Dreamer convinced me that *later* would always be better than *now*, that *someday* is where life will really happen and high school is just something we have to get through before we can live our real lives.

The Hiding—Listening to the Voice of the Dreamer

When I first got married, I worked hard to create my own little heaven on earth: cozy brown leather furniture in the living room, organized kitchen, colorful cookbooks, and clean counters. I loved my married, decorating, ministry-filled, small-group-meeting, money-budgeting, movie-watching, Starbucks life. I had finally arrived! Still, it wasn't enough.

Every year we travel to Hilton Head Island for vacation with our family. We stay in a condo under the oak trees with Spanish moss hanging lazy low from their heavy branches. It's a beautiful place to dream. As we walked down to the harbor one evening, we saw a boat we'd never seen before. I'd been coming to this spot for twelve years and my husband for all his life, and neither of us had ever seen a boat in the harbor even close to that big.

The boat's name was *Never Enough*, and the irony was not lost on anyone watching.

The crew dressed in khakis and fancy shirts in the daytime, and at dusk we saw them in their black ties. We could hear the excitement from where we stood as the yacht slowly made her way around the smaller boats. She moved slow, heavy, regal. And I wished I was there, part of the buzz and glitz and mystery.

But not really. Because as I lazily looped my arm through John's and we meandered back to our beach house, I realized that this life I live is someone else's "boat"—they look and long and wish for this. And so do I, until I remember I have it. That glamour life doesn't really exist, and the ones who chase it quickly discover *it isn't really there*. Whoever named the boat knew that. No matter how good life is, no matter how much stuff we have, no matter how well our physical needs are met, we will always long for more. This tangible life is never enough, not really.

The voice of the Dreamer often pushes us to escape. When we listen to her voice, our dreams are held captive. We dream things shaped by heaven but twisted by the world, things of escape and vacation and eternal lounging. Writer Sam McLoughlin talks about his perspective on life and dreaming as he sat on the deck of a cruise ship:

> We've been taught by countless advertisements and inspiring testimonials that this will be the experience of a lifetime: getting sun-burnt with a belly full of bacon as a band plays Jimmy Buffet tunes. This is the dream, the end-goal, the destination that consumer society provides for us: a retirement at sea. But there is so much more to life, to being fully alive, than this. . . . This is the challenge that faces me and the rest of us creatives daily—to not give into the rhythms of complacency in our everyday lives. To not settle for the dreams that society chooses for us. To look beyond, and dream up something big. This is the beginning.[1]

I started a dream list in high school, and on it I had things like Hawaiian vacations, beach lounging, New York City shopping, and big Italian lunches on a rocky coast. I dreamed of being a dancer on Broadway or a bakery chef. I dreamed of being tan. Swedish. Fluent in Spanish. I dreamed ridiculous, impossible, beautiful dreams.

The world and the movies push us to believe that a dream come true is a life of freedom to do whatever we want: lounge on the beach, live in a mansion, escape the trouble of the world or the difficulties of daily life. We are told a dream come true means finding the love of a man, having the ultimate job, traveling the world.

In his book *Desire*, John Eldredge says this: "God must take away the heaven we create, or it will become our hell. . . . I haven't wanted to be an eternal person. I've wanted to find life here somehow."[2]

It's been four months since I first saw *Never Enough* floating slowly in the harbor, and every time I see a movie star on the cover of a magazine or daydream about jumping on a plane to Paris, I think about how she may have been the biggest yacht in our harbor, but she's not the biggest yacht in the world, not by far. When you strive to be the biggest and best, the smartest and wisest and most interesting, your goal will always be frustrated with bigger and better, smarter and wiser, and much more interesting. And so there is an innocent comfort and safety in humility, in receiving what this day gives, and in knowing that none of it originates with me.

There is a difference between the dreams fed to me by this world and the ones placed within me by the hand of God. Somewhere deep down I dream of being endlessly patient, overwhelmingly kind, able to give away money by the bucketfuls. I dream of making a big difference, of beautiful things for the future, of not being afraid. And this dreaming is a part of me, of how God made me. These kinds of dreams are not meant to stay dreams. They are there for a reason, and God wants to bring them out of me, to have his dream for me infuse my dreams with his greatness. Otherwise I will always be hoping for something better, waiting for later to come. Our imaginative God invites us to embrace these right-now moments instead of waiting to live them later.

The Finding—On Hearing God's Voice

We were created to live right-now lives. Do you dream of making a difference in the world? Look around. The world will show up in your backyard, at the game on Friday night, in your chemistry class, on the back deck with your family. What are you waiting for? You don't always have to wait to live your dreams later; you can live them *now*.

Do you dream of falling in love, getting married, and having babies? Begin now to learn who you are and how God made you. Believe him for the big things as well as the small. Trust that he has good things in mind for your future. And know that surrendering your dreams to him doesn't mean they won't come true.

Do you dream of becoming an actress? A writer? A doctor or teacher or missionary? Tell him. He already knows, and chances are you dream those things because he has uniquely gifted you for them in some way you may not even be able to imagine right now.

A dream come true may look strangely ordinary in many ways—think of Jesus living for thirty years and working as a carpenter before he even began his ministry. His ministry only lasted three years, and he only had a precious few followers. But can you think of anyone who has had a greater impact on humanity? Having our dreams fulfilled may not mean stages and microphones and luxury. In fact, it usually doesn't mean that.

But what could be less risky than surrendering our dreams to the Dream Maker? Do you think it's possible that he dreams big for you too? Maybe even bigger than you could ever imagine?

The voice of the Dreamer whispers words such as *Later. Someday. Hopefully. If only. Just wait.* I wonder if Mary was a dreamer too? We talked about her before, but I can't help bringing her up again. At fifteen, she and Joseph were already engaged. I wonder if she dreamed about their life together, their wedding, what it would be like. I'm certain her dreams didn't include an unplanned pregnancy or a baby with a death sentence before she and Joseph even said "I do."

God's dreams for Mary were bigger than the dreams Mary could have had for herself. Her dreams may have been sweet, but his dreams were epic. And when you read the way Mary responded to the angel when he told her what was going to happen, it seems like perhaps she was ready and open for God's dream for her. "'I am the Lord's servant,' Mary answered. 'May your word to me be fulfilled'" (Luke 1:38 NIV). She didn't get mad that God seemed to be changing the plan. She basically said, "Awesome. Here we go!"

God made the world and he made you to go in it. His work is the work of an artist, and you are his unique handiwork. You are designed with purpose, love, and intention. He has placed eternity into your heart: a longing to be loved, to be known, to make a difference, to believe. He puts the need there, and then he is the One who meets it.

A New Kind of Hiding

When we listen to the voice of the Dreamer and hide behind our somedays, we miss out on the gifts of today. You don't have to wait for later or worry that your dreams will never come true. Offer yourself in reckless abandon to your loving Father, the heavenly Dream Weaver.

Consider the lilies of the field. Lilies are called to grow and be beautiful. And God clothes them, these little flowers that are here today and gone tomorrow. How much more will he take care of you?

Why are you worried about clothing? Observe how the lilies of the field grow; they do not toil nor do they spin, yet I say to you that not even Solomon in all his glory clothed himself like one of these. But if God so clothes the grass of the field, which is alive today and tomorrow is thrown into the furnace, will He not much more clothe you? (Matt. 6:28–30)

If he brings beauty into the world through these flowers, how much more will he allow wonder and beauty and miracles to be produced in us, through us, from his hand? When we allow ourselves to dream, God takes sweet delight in reaching into those dreams and grabbing by the fistful—to shape, to mold, to change, and to bring out the beautiful.

So what does it look like for a Dreamer to find her safe place in Christ, to live life as though she trusts him to bring out the beautiful in her?

Believe that God placed his dreams in you. Part of life is learning how God is calling those dreams to come out. We have been given everything we need for life and godliness (2 Peter 1:3), but we don't dare experience it all. There are big dreams of great influence, and small dreams also of great influence. God sees them all, and he calls us out of our fear and into the dream.

Being a believer in Jesus isn't about doing something you hate because that would be the greatest sacrifice for God. No, it is about becoming and learning who God made you to be. You don't have to pretend to like certain things or be a certain way. One college major is not more pleasing to God than another. He made each one of us with the flair of an artist, yet sometimes we insist upon falling into the same predictable molds. Could it be possible that the thing you really want to do is the thing you were actually made to do?

Believe that beauty comes from brokenness. Nobody likes this one, but it may be the most important. Sometimes a beautiful life comes out of a beautiful dream, and sometimes it comes when our own dream dies. Is it possible that God can still bring out the beauty? Jesus says yes; fruit comes when the seed is planted and broken and dies. God's biggest story is built upon beauty made, then destroyed, then remade better. There is bondage *but then comes freedom.* There is blindness *but then comes sight.* There is death *but then comes resurrection.*

Believe God wants good things for you. Jeremiah 29:11 says God has plans for you, plans filled with hope and a future. Hold on to that beautiful hope, no matter what kind of ugliness greets you in the morning, no matter what kind of disappointments may show up at your door.

Hope has a name: *Jesus.* Invite him into your dreaming. Let him come in and sit down in the living room of your future. Believe that he has gone before you to prepare a place for you in the world, not just for what you will be when you grow up, but for what you are this afternoon. God is not confined to time and space like we are. The future is now, and he is waiting, giddy to show up beautiful in this moment.

I can't imagine a better picture of a graceful life than one of a dancer. She listens to the truth of the music and her body moves to the rhythm she hears in that moment. She does not imagine a song she heard yesterday and try to dance to that one, concerning herself with things already in the past. She doesn't wish for a better, newer song, concerning herself with things yet to come.

How awkward and impossible it would be for her to ignore the music playing and try a different dance instead? A graceful dancer surrenders herself to the right-now music rather than wish for a different beat. She takes the truth of the harmony and moves in her own unique way.

Jesus sings his truth songs over us, moment by moment. When we trust him, listen to him, believe his words as truth right now, our life song can be unique and graceful too.

Truths to Remember When the Dreamer Begins to Speak

Your dreams are safe in the hands of the heavenly Dream Weaver. "'For I know the plans that I have for you,' declares the LORD, 'plans for welfare and not for calamity to give you a future and a hope'" (Jer. 29:11).

Receive your dreams as a gift. You have been made with purpose and intention. As you walk with God in the daily minute, your dreams will rise up to the surface. "Delight yourself in the LORD; and He will give you the desires of your heart" (Ps. 37:4).

God can make broken dreams into beautiful things. "The Spirit of the Lord God is upon me, because the Lord has anointed me to bring good news to the afflicted; He has sent me to bind up the brokenhearted, to proclaim liberty to captives and freedom to prisoners . . . to grant those who mourn in Zion, giving them a garland instead of ashes, the oil of gladness instead of mourning, the mantle of praise instead of a spirit of fainting" (Isa. 61:1–3).

the beloved

A Different Kind of Hiding

Love makes your soul crawl out from its hiding place.

—*Zora Neale Hurston*[1]

I saw him standing with a group of freshman girls, his hands tucked deep in his jeans pockets, his blond hair nearly reaching his lashes. The girls were giggly and chatty around him, and I didn't realize until later they weren't really talking with him, just near him. I brought my camera that night to youth group, hoping to document some of the ever-changing student faces for our group website at the beginning of the semester. When I approached this small group, I assumed they all knew each other. But when I asked for them to group together so I could get a shot, the guy froze up and looked at me terrified, like I had asked him to stand up and sing naked. He shook his head, small and pleading, and so I took the photo of the three girls without him. *Boys*, I thought to myself as I walked away. *They're so weird.*

Later that night, John came home and told me about a student who came that night who had never, ever been to church before. He had quit smoking pot three weeks ago, and he came with a friend because his family recently discovered his mom had cancer. He needed something real, something true, something other than what he already had. And so he came to our youth group.

I'm sure you've guessed by now that I'm talking about the awkward, anti-photo, blond guy. Before he learned of his mom's cancer, life went on as usual. It wasn't until he realized he didn't have the resources to deal with his situation that he sought some answers.

We will listen to the good girl voices until what they tell us doesn't work for us anymore. We will continue to try hard and to do right and to work tirelessly until we come to a place of recognizing we can never do enough.

At an early age, I understood how Jesus came to rescue us. He came to save sinners. He came for the lost. He came to heal sick people and to raise dead people and to die for the sins of everyone.

Never once did I consider he also came to save me from myself. I'm a good girl who has done some good things and has mostly good intentions for the world around me. What harm could I do to myself? But then I think of the effort and the work. I think of the worry that keeps me up at night and the fear that perhaps I've not done enough. I think of the way I compare myself to others and the pain that comes when I look for worth and security from my appearance or my friendships or my successes. I consider how painful it is when I fail. And all I'm left with are two measly handfuls of self-effort as I stand weak in front of my mountain-sized problems. I hang my head low and feel in my heart an overwhelming sense of shame. I am not enough. I cannot get it right. I cannot handle this life.

And so when I came to a point where I began to realize how very helpless I was to live this Christian life, I was overwhelmed. I felt hopeless to ever change or be different. I sat across from a trusted friend and counselor one summer. Slumped over in a worn-out chair, I confessed, "I don't know how to *not* be this way." These voices, these masks, this life motivated by fear was all I knew. I wanted him to unveil a five-, ten-, or hundred-step program to teach me what to do and how to live real and free. I would do anything.

A small smile played its way across his face, and what he said next was the most freeing, simple, and life-changing thing that has yet been said to me. "You're *not* this way. This may be how you cope, but this is not who you are."

This is not who you are.

You are not merely a rule-following, reputation-making, image-maintaining, responsible, intellectual good girl. You are not just a girl who needs to try harder, do better, be more, look good, be perfect. You are not the boring one, the responsible one, the counselor, the peacemaker, the background friend, or the problem solver. These hiding places may have been helping you cope, but they are not who you are.

These good girl voices challenge your identity. They say, *We know who you really are, so you better hide before someone else finds out.* I hope you are beginning to hear a hushed, holy voice from the background rise up to meet you right where you are. (See these expanded in the "From Good to Graceful" chart on pp. 165–66.)

The Actress says, "Perform!"

But there is a restful voice that says, "Accepted!"

The Girl Next Door says, "Impress."

But there is a calming voice that says, "For am I now seeking the favor of men, or of God? Or am I striving to please men? If I were still trying to please men, I would not be a bond-servant of Christ" (Gal. 1:10).

The Activist declares, "Impact!"

A saving voice sings, "In the world you will have tribulation, but take courage; I have overcome the world" (John 16:33).

The Heroine repeats her mantra, "Responsibility."

Jesus issues an invitation: "Come to Me, all who are weary and heavy-laden, and I will give you rest" (Matt. 11:28).

The Bystander whispers, "Stay invisible."

A new voice beckons, "You are the light of the world. A city set on a hill cannot be hidden; nor does anyone light a lamp and put it under a basket, but on the lampstand, and it gives light to all who are in the house" (Matt. 5:14–15).

The Judge demands, "Follow the rules."

A grace-filled voice urges, "You are not under law but under grace" (Rom. 6:14).

The Intellectual challenges, "You have to be right."

A calming voice says, "Cease *striving*, and know that I am God" (Ps. 46:10).

The Dreamer sighs, "Someday."

A better voice whispers, "Today."

When God thinks of you, one simple word comes to his mind—beloved.

You are not the second choice.

Jesus came to save you from self-effort. He didn't just die for your sin to give you forgiveness; he rose up again to give you life. And so he beckons you, "Come."

Arise my darling, my beautiful one, and come with me. See! The winter is past; the rains are over and gone. Flowers appear on the earth; the season of singing has come, the cooing of doves is heard in our land. The fig tree forms its early fruit; the blossoming vines spread their fragrance. Arise, come, my darling; my beautiful one, come with me. (Song of Sol. 2:10–14)

Solomon speaks of his beloved this way. Jesus does too. And his beloved is you.

You have the ability to choose which voices you believe. You have the freedom to decide where you are going to hide: behind your good girl identities or in the truth of your identity as beloved in Christ. And the only way to hide in Christ is to receive him as a gift. Not just for salvation like when you were little, but for every day, this minute, this situation.

There are no action steps when it comes to receiving. It isn't an algebra formula and there aren't sure-fire steps or 100 percent success rates. You can't measure the results of receiving, but you can certainly watch their effects.

What It Means to Receive

My favorite movie as a girl was *The Wizard of Oz*. I thought Judy Garland's Dorothy was the most beautiful girl I had ever seen. I idolized Dorothy. She was innocent, loving, and kind. That voice, that dress, that dog, those shoes! She had it all. Years later when I heard movie commentators describe her as chubby, I was so confused. Chubby? Hardly. To me, she was perfect.

I've thought about this movie a lot as I have grown up. The Scarecrow wanted a brain; the Tin Man, a heart. The Lion longed for courage, and all Dorothy wanted was to find a way home. They followed yellow brick roads, ran from flying monkeys, and even risked their lives to get the broomstick of the Wicked Witch just like the Wizard—who really was no wizard at all—asked them to. They did it all because they longed for something they did not have. In the end we learn along with them that they had it all along;

they just didn't know it. They worked, they chased, they strived, and they feared, all in an effort to get what had already been given.

After all, the Scarecrow was often the one to devise all the plans; the Tin Man rusted from crying real, heartfelt tears; and the Lion found the courage to save Dorothy, all before they even met the Wizard. Dorothy was the most obvious of all. She couldn't take a step without being aware of those sparkly, ruby slippers. Still, when she finally saw Glinda, she cried out for help and was told she always had the power to go back to Kansas. The slippers she had all along were the very means by which she would make her way home. But she didn't know it.

Knowing what you have makes all the difference. We have been given everything we need for life and godliness, but if we don't know it, we will never experience the reality of it. And just like Dorothy and those ruby slippers, as a believer in Jesus, no matter what you do, you have already been given everything you need for this life.

Knowing the truth is essential. Dorothy walked all over Oz and Munchkin Land in those ruby slippers without knowing they were her ticket home. At the end of the movie, when Glinda finally told her she always had the power to go back to Kansas, she had to actually *let the truth be true*. She had the *letting power*. And so do we.

Colossians 3:15 says, "Let the peace of Christ rule in your hearts." When I hear that word *peace*, I imagine woven crowns of dandelions on top of the unbrushed hair of barefoot hippies. I think of cliché beauty pageant answers and two-fingered peace signs flashed halfheartedly as we pose for pictures. But those images of peace are watered down versions of what peace means in the Bible.

The world *rule* in verse fifteen literally means "to act as umpire."[2] Championships teeter on the call of an umpire. Scholarships, futures, money, effort, and years of practice are often insulted with one bad call. We could go so far as to say that dreams ride on the backs of umpires. That's a little extreme, but the point is that in sports, we need to trust our umpires. When we don't, the game gets ugly.

Anyone who is called an umpire should be trustworthy, impartial, and able to handle the pressure. Colossians 3:15 invites us to let peace be our umpire.

> um·pire: one having authority to decide finally a controversy or question between parties: as a: one appointed to decide between arbitrators who have disagreed[3]

And if it is too weird to imagine something as abstract as *peace* being our umpire, here is something else the Bible says about peace.

> But now in Christ Jesus you who formerly were far off have been brought near by the blood of Christ. *For He Himself is our peace*, who made both groups into one and broke down the barrier of the dividing wall. (Eph. 2:13–14, emphasis added)

Jesus is our peace. And peace is to be our umpire. An umpire is someone who decides between two parties who disagree—the fake and the real, the fear and the love, the voice of the good girl and the voice of God. Peace stands between God and the good girl, then turns to look you straight in the eye and ask permission to do what peace does best: give rest. God offers his peace—his Son—to act as our umpire, to release us from having to be the authority and keep it together. But we have to let peace be peaceful within us. We have to receive this peace. It isn't an easy thing to do, but here is what it can look like.

For the words you have to listen to that you wish didn't exist, words like *cancer* or *divorce* or *funeral* or *God has a plan, you know*—when you wish his plan had a lot less broken and a lot more whole—know that you have a Healer who is close by. Let him comfort you.

For the times when you make the team, when those girls finally understand you, when that relationship you were worried about takes a turn for the better and you find yourselves laughing together again—know that you have a Maker who laughs with you. Let him celebrate you.

For when you question the whole thing, wondering, *How could a good God let this happen?* For when you don't know why you try so hard. For when you don't have answers to all those questions and just want to put off trusting him until after you watch a chick flick while eating some Java Chip ice cream—know that you have a God who waits patiently with you, for you. Let him escort you.

For when you prepare to go off to college and you know you are supposed to feel grown up but you just feel like a kid. For when you are terrified that you'll get it wrong, choose the wrong major, find the wrong friends—know that you have a God who has gone before you. He is already there, at school, in the dorm, among you. Let him welcome you.

For when you feel invisible and wonder if anyone, *anyone* in the world could possibly understand you. For when you want to know that you matter, that your life has purpose, that your feelings are not crazy—know that you have a Friend who sees you. Let him know you.

For when you completely mess up, and not in a cute way. For when you open your mouth and betray a friend, when you tell a secret and immediately regret it, when you spew ugliness and judgment with your mouth or in your heart—know that you have a God who stands in the gap for you. Let him remake you.

Let him. This peace named Jesus does not force himself in. He stands at the door and he knocks. At salvation, yes, but also on Tuesday. He knocks on the way to school, at the game Friday night, at the cafeteria table, during your driver's test, while you study for the SAT, when you look into that boy's eyes, as you laugh with your best friend, while you hurt over your broken heart. He stands with you in every circumstance and invites you to welcome his peace into it.

Where the Letting Happens

At the beginning of this book, we talked about the many layers we have on us. There's the skin, the part you can see. There is also more that you can't see, like bones and organs, but that stuff is all what makes up our body. It's how we touch, see, smell, taste, and hear. Everyone has a body.

But there's more, and everyone knows it. Because you can have all those things and still be dead. What makes a person alive?

Life comes from somewhere invisible, a place that is real even though you can't see it and has impact even though you can't touch it. Somehow, we *think*. We have thoughts and we ruminate over them. We read books and we experience things in our imagination. We can learn and we can dream and we can imagine things that aren't there. We have the ability to create things with thoughts alone.

We have a *mind*.

We also have memories, and those memories of our past influence decisions we make in our future. We can see two choices or fifty choices, and we can think and then decide. We can say yes or no or maybe or wait or later or we'll see.

We have a *will*.

Those memories and those decisions don't happen in a vacuum. They affect us. They matter to us. We can categorize them as important or unimportant. We have the ability to communicate and reason and interact with people. And sometimes people are the most glorious in all of creation and we just can't wait to be around them. They make us feel good, happy, joyful, peaceful, and delighted. But sometimes those same people inflict wounds deeper than any weapon can. Their words cut and we bleed invisibly. And the pain is almost physical, except that it isn't. All of that can happen within a day's time, and we end up feeling as though we've both flown to the heights of heaven and been thrown into the ugly bowels of hell. All in one day.

It is because we have *emotions*.

If we all agree that we have this mind, this will, and these emotions, then where do they all live? They can't be my body, because everything that is my body can be touched, held, seen.

We call this invisible self the soul. Everyone has a soul, because everyone can think, choose, and feel. But there is still more. If there weren't, then our entire experience of life would be based only upon our body (what we look like) and our soul (what we think, choose, and feel). There is one more blessed truth to consider as we think about how fearfully and wonderfully we have been made.

We have a body to interact with our environment, a soul to interact and understand ourselves and other people, and we also have a *spirit* where we interact with and understand God. We are not just body, just soul, or just spirit. Our entire being was put together by God. We need all three to be whole.

> Now may the God of peace Himself sanctify you entirely; and may your *spirit* and soul and body be preserved complete, without blame at the coming of our Lord Jesus Christ. (1 Thess. 5:23, emphasis added)

Ending with the Beginning

Remember our friends in the Garden? We left the man and the woman way back in chapter 2. We left them there, having listened to the voice of the enemy, eaten the fruit from the one tree they weren't supposed to eat from, knowing what they did was wrong, and doing the only thing they knew to do: hide. Do you remember what God told them would happen if they ate from the tree?

> The LORD God commanded the man, saying, "From any tree of the garden you may eat freely; but from the tree of the knowledge of good and evil you shall not eat, for in the day that you eat from it you will surely die." (Gen. 2:16–17)

But did they die physically? Not yet, even though their choice set in motion the dying process that wouldn't happen until years later. In that moment, they still had their working bodies. Did their souls die? No, they definitely still had emotions and thoughts and wills of their own. So what died?

If our bodies are how we relate to one another and our souls are how we experience those relationships and understand ourselves, then our *spirits* are the invisible place where we relate with God. That day in the Garden, the man and woman's spirits died—that invisible place where they were connected to their God. And so every human after that was born into Adam, into death, with a dead spirit.

The only way to bring the spirit to life is to admit it is dead and receive the One who is life. When my spirit meets God's Holy Spirit, life is made available. We call that salvation. We have been saved from a self-dependent life. We have been saved from having to make life work on our own.

Now we have a choice. We can either receive our truth from our appearance by looking at our body, we can receive our truth from our emotions by responding to what our soul says, or we can believe that God's Spirit is now united with our spirit and receive our truth from him. We can either continue to listen to the voices of the good girl or lean our ear heavy toward the voice of God.

That's why Jesus came to earth—to restore the life that was lost in the Garden, to provide a way for humankind to be reunited with God. But have you ever wondered, *If Jesus came to save the world, then what about all the people who lived and died before he came?* Good question, and the answer is simple: faith.

The people who lived from the Garden all the way up to that silent night in Bethlehem, they put their faith in the hope of a Savior *who would one day come.* Today, we put our faith in the hope of a Savior *who already came.*

Either way, it's all faith. And the God who formed the world with a holy word has been providing a way for us since the beginning of time. It started in the Garden, when Adam and Eve hid in the bushes and he called out to them, "Where are you?" He asked them; he asks us as well.

Adam and Eve's response of guilt over what they had done was exactly right. They sinned, and they were guilty. But if all they felt was guilt, they would have run at top speed back to the arms of their Father. Guilt wasn't their only problem.

Like when my sweet friend Sarah from our youth group told me she went to a party instead of staying at her friend's house like she was supposed to. She came to me and asked if I thought she needed to confess that to her parents. If she felt only guilty, she would have run to her mom, confessing in a gush of *I'm so sorry I lied!* But she didn't want to do that because she felt more than guilt. She felt shame.

That's what Adam and Eve felt too. So they made themselves a hiding place where they thought they wouldn't be found. But they needed so much more than just a place to hide; they needed forgiveness and life. God lovingly, graciously, and miraculously provided both.

He did not let them remain hidden behind the masks they fashioned for themselves. He did not let the voice of their enemy have the final say. Instead, he killed an innocent animal, right there in the Garden, to cover Adam and Eve—the first sacrifice for sin that pointed to the future sacrifice of Christ. Because of his great love and compassion, God provided an escape for humankind by holding back the wrath they actually deserved.

We call this mercy.

But simply providing escape isn't actually enough. Mercy, as beautiful as it is, is only protection. So God made garments of skin for them from the sacrificed animal. In doing so, he gave them something they did not deserve.

We call this grace.

God took away the hiding place they crafted for themselves and made for them a new one on his terms.

Mercy protects. Grace provides.

A few thousand years later, he would send Jesus, whom the Bible calls the second Adam. He lived a full human life, depending on his Father in all the ways the first Adam failed to do. "For the sin of this one man, Adam, caused death to rule over many. But even greater is God's wonderful grace and his gift of righteousness, for all who receive it will live in triumph over sin and death through this one man, Jesus Christ" (Rom. 5:17 NLT). In the person of Jesus, mercy and grace show up perfect and pour out all over us.

Adam and Eve were right about one thing: after they sinned, they needed a place to hide. But God did not let them stay in hiding on their own terms, and he doesn't let us either.

The Hiding Place of Shame

One of the reasons it's so easy for us to listen to the good girl voices is because those voices appear to help us deal with our shame problem. When we see something in ourselves that isn't right—something ugly or prideful or lazy or anxious—we want nothing more than to get rid of it. If we've grown up in the church, or even if we have learned (without growing up in the church) that we are supposed to do certain things or act certain ways in order to make ourselves right, then listening to these voices makes perfect sense. They aren't telling us to do bad things; they are telling us to do good things.

Be nice.

Make good grades.

Have patience.

Serve the poor.

Don't complain.

Find the right answer.

And for the love , be a good girl.

As we try hard to do things right, we either become puffed up and prideful when we succeed, or increasingly frustrated when we don't.

The original sin in the Garden was that the man and the woman depended on themselves rather than God. That was it. They took their lives into their own hands, and in the process they lost life altogether. It's serious business trying to make life work on our own. It's what started this mess in the first place.

Do you see this connection between a self-identity and a God-identity? God takes any kind of sin very seriously, both the kind that looks really bad and the kind that looks kind of good. He would never dream of expecting us to handle this sin on our own. It's too big, too bad, too much. So he sent the law to let unbelievers know how bad it is, he sent his Son to pay for it, and he sent his Spirit to give us the authority to resist it. When we sin, guilt is the right response. Guilt is used by God to show us our need for him. Guilt is not our problem.

Guilt says I *did* wrong. (That's a good thing to know.)

Shame says I *am* wrong.

Guilt deals with behavior.

Shame deals with identity.

Guilt leads to repentance.

Shame leads to hiding.

In *The Wizard of Oz*, when Dorothy, the Scarecrow, and the Tin Man meet the Cowardly Lion in the forest, the Lion tries to bite Toto, and Dorothy slaps his face and shouts, "Shame on you!" We hear phrases like that a lot—*For shame!* or *You should be ashamed of yourself!* When someone says that, they are basically saying, *You have brought disgrace upon yourself. You should feel badly and make up for it.*

Think about that word *disgrace*. The prefix *dis-* means "apart" or "away," like trying to push two magnets together. All they want to do is go apart, right? Shame and grace are the same way; shame is the literal opposite of grace.

There is no grace in shame.

And so we have a choice to make. We can believe the dark suggestion that it is up to us to get things right on our own. Or we can trust that we were made in God's image for such a time as this, and receive grace and mercy from his hand.

The Hiding Place of Grace

When God killed the animal in the Garden, he showed mercy to Adam and Eve. He did the same thing for us by sending the innocent Christ, showing mercy by punishing him with the punishment meant for us. We know about this one. We sing about this one. Jesus died on the cross. Got it.

But there is another reason for this sacrifice, one that is more difficult to understand and, frankly, less believable. In the Garden, God not only showed his mercy by holding back the punishment the man and woman deserved; he also showed them grace by giving them garments from the animal, offering something they *didn't* deserve.

You celebrate it though you may not realize it. Once a year on Easter, we remember how Christ's physical body died, was buried, and rose up again. We also celebrate it at the communion table where we drink the cup (representing his blood) and eat the bread (representing his body). But other than these two remembrances, the resurrected Christ doesn't get much airtime in our minds.

Good girls know about the forgiveness, but we aren't as familiar with the life. And so we live trying hard to get the life by doing the best we can.

It's true that Christ died for us. But it is also true that *we died with him*. And if we died with him, then when he was buried, we were buried. And when he rose up from the dead, we rose up from the dead. It sounds crazy, but the Bible says it's true:

Therefore we have been buried with Him through baptism into death, so that as Christ was raised from the dead through the glory of the Father, so we too might walk in newness of life. For if we have become united with Him in the likeness of His death, certainly we shall also be in the likeness of His resurrection, knowing this, that our old self was crucified with Him, in order that our body of sin might be done away with, so that we would no longer be slaves to sin; for he who has died is freed from sin. Now if we have died with Christ, we believe that we shall also live with Him. (Rom. 6:4–8)

So who cares, right? What difference does it make? That sounds so ancient, so Bible time-y, so irrelevant. But this makes every difference for our everyday life. It really does. Because now we do not have to manufacture our own safe places. We have been placed into safety. "For you have died and your life is hidden with Christ in God" (Col. 3:3). This is a different kind of hiding than the one we have practiced as good girls.

When we really begin to see and embrace the safe place where we dwell, there is new hope for the entire human race to breathe a collective sigh of sweet relief. God, through Jesus, provided a better way, and because of that, there is a new way to live. It is the way of trust, of dependence, of leaning hard into the One who holds all things together even when they fall apart.

the God who set her free

The Freedom of Being Found

When I am dangerously tired I can be very, very busy
and look very, very important but be unable to hear the
quiet, sure voice of the One who calls me the beloved.

—*Ruth Haley Barton*[1]

In the midst of an active, blurry week, John came home from a
walk with a friend who asked him this question: *Are you willing
to be more and do less?* As he told me about their conversation, his
words stopped me in my dinner-making, clothes-washing, nose-
wiping tracks. My doing far outweighed my being.

Be more. Do less. It sounds as blissful as it does unrealistic. You
may find yourself thinking, *That's great and all, but I have college applications to fill out, AP Euro homework to finish, lacrosse
practice to go to, that group project to start, and oh yeah, I have
no money for gas, no patience for my family, and no life because*

I'm so busy. There is no room for rest, for stillness, for quiet. The words repeat like a drumbeat in the background.

Do. Act. Work. Produce.

The voice of God becomes a distant memory. The voice of the good girl speaks clear as a bell. Instead of feeling like the *be*loved, I feel more like the *do*loved.

Then I remember Jesus. He reminds me that remaining in him means refusing to get up from his lap. When it seems like the situation calls for me to stand up and take charge, Jesus gives me permission to remain still, if only on the inside—to trust deeply and fully that he will be strong on my behalf. Even when it seems impossible. Even when it's counterintuitive. Even if it means I will look weak. To remain in him means to let God be God. And there is that word again: *let.*

> Abide in Me, and I in you. As the branch cannot bear fruit of itself unless it abides in the vine, so neither can you unless you abide in Me. I am the vine, you are the branches; he who abides in Me and I in him, he bears much fruit, for apart from Me you can do nothing. (John 15:1–5)

The job of a branch is not to make life happen but to abide, *remain* in the tree. To remain means to stay where you already are. No need to get up and try to find that which you already have. And so there is another voice inviting you to abide in him and rest.

He renews, restores, and redeems. In the inspired words of Sarah Young, "He bends time in your favor."[2] In a day that seems impossibly packed to overflowing with your to-do list, he can multiply time and space like loaves and fishes beside the sea. And the gentle rhythm of truth rises from within.

Be. Trust. Receive. Respond.

When I live as though I believe that's true, activity doesn't stop. Rather, it takes on new life. It means purposing in my heart not to worry. It means pausing before I send that angry text to consider the peace that Jesus brings. It means taking three minutes before I start that research paper to ask him to sit with me. It means listening for his voice before I speak, learning the difference between fear and love, and letting Jesus lead me into the next situation. It means holding my plans with an open hand and a willing heart. Even in the midst of lots of activity, our souls have permission to rest.

Learning to listen to and believe God's voice means learning to refuse the voice of fear. All the good girl voices we've talked about in this book are motivated by fear.

The Actress fears she isn't doing enough.

The Girl Next Door fears what people think.

The Activist fears she isn't making a difference.

The Heroine fears her weakness.

The Bystander fears she is invisible.

The Judge fears she won't get it right.

The Intellectual fears criticism.

The Dreamer fears she is missing out.

Fear isn't necessarily something we should ignore. That would just be another form of hiding. God gives us the courage to face those fears and then invites us to move toward him in the midst of them. Standing with him, we have a choice. We don't have to believe these voices. As believers in the person of Jesus, we can instead listen to his voice. So how do we know what his voice is saying?

In John 10, people questioned Jesus's authority. Even though he told them over and over, they still didn't understand who he was. One of them even said to him,

"How long will You keep us in suspense? If You are the Christ, tell us plainly." Jesus answered them, "I told you, and you do not believe; the works that I do in My Father's name, these testify of Me. But you do not believe because you are not of My sheep. My sheep hear My voice, and I know them, and they follow Me; and I give eternal life to them, and they will never perish; and no one will snatch them out of My hand." (John 10:24–28)

Jesus could have said, "I told you, and you do not do anything for me. You don't work for me or serve me or please me or follow me." But instead he says, "I told you, and you do not *believe*." And there it is again, that word *believe*. The order of what Jesus says here is so important.

> **My sheep hear my voice.** We are his sheep, and he speaks to us! We receive truth from him.
>
> **I know them.** He knows us inside, outside, and upside down. We have to let this be true in our experience. So far, no action has taken place except the action of belief.
>
> **They follow me.** Here's some action. First we hear his voice, then we remain in the truth that he knows us. Only after hearing from God and believing he is trustworthy are we able to respond—follow him.
>
> **I give them eternal life.** And now we're back to what Jesus does. He gives eternal life. What is eternal life? The Bible calls Jesus himself eternal life. He gives us the gift of himself, the gift of enough. The only way we can follow Jesus is by the strength and life of Jesus himself. We can't follow him by our own strength of trying hard, but only by relying on his eternal life within us.
>
> **They will never die.** Death has no power over those who believe. Paul says, "To live is Christ, and to die is gain" (Phil. 1:21).
>
> **No one will take them from me.** We are safe forever. "For you have died and your life is hidden with Christ in God" (Col. 3:3).

Because of Jesus,

> You are enough.
> You are secure.
> You are the salt of the earth.
> You are cared for.
> You are seen.
> You are forgiven.
> You are free.
> You have hope.

God is love, and that means you are loved.
God is peace, and his peace lives in you.
God is enough, and you are filled with his enough-ness.
God is who he says he is, and he made you to be his beloved.

How to Live

So what's a girl to do, a girl who knows this truth and wants to live it out? What does it mean to respond to Jesus? Are we to copy him? Wonder what he would do in a given situation and then try to do that thing? I think it is much simpler than that.

He asks us to simply show up and be willing. Don't just get dressed and be there. Anyone can be there and still stay hidden. You can live your whole life hidden, and lots of people do.

Show up with your passion and your readiness to create and explore and take a risk. Jesus lives in you, and his life wants to come out of you. If your life is hidden with Christ, that means you are safe. That means that "neither death, nor life, nor angels, nor principalities, nor things present, nor things to come, nor powers, nor height, nor depth, nor any other created thing, will be able to separate us from the love of God, which is in Christ Jesus our Lord" (Rom.

8:38–39). The freedom of being found is that you can show up as you, not as a cleaned-up version of you or an exaggerated try-hard copy of someone else. You can show up with all of your flaws and your ridiculous quirks and imperfections. When you do that, you worship.

What comes to mind when you hear that word, *worship*? If you're like me, you think singing. Maybe reading your Bible out loud. Maybe you picture your church sanctuary or worship center. God never intended for us to refer to church as a building, and he never intended worship to be reduced to something that happens during a church service. His church is his people, and worship is what we do.

Perhaps you're like me a little bit, and you tend to divide up your days into categories: school, work, service, exercise, church, small group, practice, homework, chores, friends, and if you're lucky, rest. We are always the same person doing those things, but they take different kinds of effort and personality on our part. What can happen is we see worship as one of those categories too, and it doesn't even seem like a very important one.

I'm beginning to discover that worship simply means responding to Jesus in everything. Breathing can be worship when I know it comes from him. Hanging out with friends is worship when we recognize that friendship is a gift and we treat it as such. Cleaning your room can be worship when you know that Jesus is the One who gives you the patience and the ability to finish. Walk the dog, run the marathon, enjoy your friends, paint your room, have a sleepover, and know that all these things are gifts that come from his hand.

You can act like a fool with your girlfriends and laugh until you can't breathe. As you laugh, wait for love, long for home, pour out your hearts and hopes and fears and longings; as you create with words and photos and food and paint and clothes, know that all these things are beautiful acts of worship.

But we don't call it that, do we? We call those things *living*.

When the Spirit of the living God lives inside of you, then your living is also your worship. What else would it be?

And whatever you do [no matter what it is] in word or deed, do everything in the name of the Lord Jesus and in [dependence upon] His Person giving praise to God the Father through Him. (Col. 3:17 AMP)

When we depend on Jesus, when we know we can't but he can, we worship. It is so much bigger, yet so much simpler, than we let it be. When we let peace rule, we worship. When we receive God's truth, we worship. When we remain in him, we worship. This is

at are true is
ntic and real
t doesn't feel
I believe that

You are your
feeling like a
t the fact that
Day or on your
gular days, you
You don't feel
like one. It just is.

It is difficult to believe something that doesn't feel true. But it isn't impossible.

You are the daughter of the King. I know you don't feel like it, but that doesn't make it any less true.

You are created in the image of God. I know it doesn't feel that way, but that doesn't mean it isn't true.

You are safe even when you don't feel safe.

You are accepted even when you don't feel acceptable.
You are loved even when you don't feel loveable.
You are beloved even when you feel invisible.
You are graceful even when you feel disgraceful.

It's hard enough to believe the truth when it doesn't feel true, like on a regular rainy Wednesday. But what about in the midst of heartache, when someone has hurt you so deeply that you don't know which way is up? What does it mean to set your mind on truth in the midst of failure, either yours or someone else's? What do you do when you are worried and bothered and don't know what's true anymore?

My dear friend Annie Downs wrote a book called *Perfectly Unique*,[3] and in it she talks about a particularly hurtful encounter she had with a so-called friend who basically spewed every unkind thought she had ever had about Annie right out into her face.

Annie was devastated. So much so that she couldn't think straight. She was tempted to take every word and soak it right up into her very self, to take it all in as true and let all those horrible things define her. But she made a different choice. She went to a few trusted friends, girls who had known her for a long time, girls who prayed for her. She went through each unkind word line by line with these friends, and she asked them, "Is there any truth to this unkind word spoken of me?" And her friends sat with her and spoke truth to her. Together they waded through the murky waters of relationship.

Annie fought for truth that day. She heard competing voices, and she made a decision to find truth in the midst of the chaos. Two things about that story that I love. One, even though Annie had a so-called friend who was hateful to her, she had *other* friends who loved her with Jesus's kind of love. Do you have friends like that? Friends who will speak truth to you in the midst of heartache?

The second thing I love about this story is that Annie asked for truth. She didn't go to her friends and have a gossip session. She launched a search for truth, stripped down to the basics. Want to know what you are to think on in the midst of the cloudy gray of heartbreak, boredom, fear, longing, or loss? God tells us in black and white:

> Finally, brethren, whatever is true, whatever is honorable, whatever is right, whatever is pure, whatever is lovely, whatever is of good repute, if there is any excellence and if anything worthy of praise, dwell on these things. (Phil. 4:8)

This doesn't mean our thoughts are to be happy all the time. We will be hurt, lonely, disappointed, sad, and angry. These emotions are what make us fully human, along with joy, happiness, excitement, love, and passion. But if you find yourself stuck in a place in your mind that you can't get out of; if you discover that you are having a hard time moving forward because you don't know what voice to believe anymore; if you have a thought, a fear, or a word spoken to you and you wonder if it is worth your time to think on, put it through the filter of Philippians 4:8.

On Hearing God's Voice

I wish I had an app for my phone that would pop up a 3-D map for my life, complete with charts and graphs and warnings clearly marked. So often, all we want as good girls is to do our very best by God, our parents, our friends. We desperately want to be pleasing to everyone; we long for nothing more than to be in the center of God's will.

Sometimes we can lose ourselves in this longing, and not in a good way. We want so much to please God that we never learn to trust him in our daily minute. We spend so much time looking at our lives from a helicopter view that we forget that Jesus came to walk among us, to eat our food and drink our water and then to offer himself as food and water to us. For today. For right now. It's the only time we've got.

Right now, maybe you pray as a habit just before you lie down to sleep. Maybe you pray before the test because you studied hard and you want to remember, or you studied only halfway and you hope for a miracle. Maybe you have a typical prayer you say before you eat your food, like the one I prayed as a kid—*Thank you, Jesus, for this food, thank you for Mommy, Daddy, Sissy, me, everybody, this day, A-men.*

But when control drips through your fingers like water, prayer starts to look a lot less like a discipline and a lot more like air. Life. Breath. Necessary. Essential. Dependence on Jesus doesn't look like a list. It may start out that way, but it won't end up that way.

Let's say you just got your driver's license and your parents buy you a car. (Woo to the hoo!) You're driving to school, and at a stoplight, you realize you're behind a girl you've seen at youth group a few times. You see a Jesus-y sticker on her bumper with some kind of Jesus-y slogan, and you can't help it, but immediately you think it's lame and a little cheesy. Then you think about the choice she must have made to actually put the Jesus bumper sticker on her car in the first place. The dialogue in your mind goes something like this:

Jesus bumper sticker. Lame. But she must be totally in love with Jesus if she would risk lameness to put a Jesus bumper sticker on the back of her car. I wonder if I would be willing to be lame for Jesus? I don't think so. {Pause.} *God, would you want me to put a Jesus bumper sticker on my car? I so hope not. But what if you do, and I'm not willing?* Oh no. I think God wants me to put a Jesus bumper sticker on my car. I really, super much don't want to do that. But why would he *not* want me to do that? It would let everyone know I'm a Christian. It would be straight up bold and uncomfortable, and isn't that what God wants? For me to be bold? And uncomfortable? This must be God's voice, because he's asking me to do something I don't want to do. He always asks me to step out from my comfort zone. {Big sigh.} But if I can't put a Jesus bumper sticker on my car, then I'm really not a very obedient Christian. It's a stupid little sticker. Some people go to foreign countries and risk their lives for God, and I'm not even willing to put a sticker on my car. What kind of a Christian isn't even willing to risk looking a little bit foolish for God?

And so we reduce God's voice to one asking us to do hard things, uncomfortable things, bold things, silly things, risky things. We think when we have an idea that we don't like or scares us or feels risky, *that must be God*. No wonder we don't want to hang out with him. No wonder we worry what he might call us to!

There is a way to filter all of those things you hear in your head, all of those ideas that you don't know if they are yours or God's, all of that shame you feel when you think you aren't willing to live the way he would want. What if we started listening first to who God says he is, then to who God says we are? After that (and only after that) will we be able to listen to what he wants us to do.

The things God asks of you may feel risky sometimes, they may require shedding your comfort zone, they may feel bold and you may not feel up to the task. But when you choose to first listen to who God says he is and then who he says you are, the task becomes yours together and not yours alone. And that makes all the difference. The battle is really fought in our minds, in what we choose to believe is true. And when we know who God is and who we are, then and only then will we be equipped to do anything at all.

On Being Found

Being found means God is with you, for you, in you, around you. He longs for you to take joy in his presence and rest in the safe place he has made for you. He doesn't want your empty willingness to be sold out for God. He isn't impressed with your grand gestures of obedience. He just wants you. And when he has you, that is the place from where decisions are made or unmade, relationships begin or end, and love wins.

You are writing your past today. Every morning when you get up, you pick up an invisible pen with your life, and you write the story you will tell to your children and their children. The story you are writing might not make sense, and it may get a little bit ugly—sometimes more than a little bit. But ugly doesn't always have to mean major rebellion or a stint in rehab. Sometimes ugly is a simple lack of faith, a tantrum on the inside, a panic in the night. There will be twists that don't make sense and turns you can't control. But there will also be wide open fields with flowers of choice and promise. You get to pick how you want to live your life.

Your moms pray for you to make good decisions. So do your small group leaders and sometimes your coaches and your chorus teachers, too. And so do I, as I write these words. I pray that the God of the universe will strengthen you according to his glorious might. Good decisions are highly recommended, but there is more to life than simply making good decisions, staying on the "right" path, and not having too many regrets.

There is more, so much more. Because in ten years, you probably will be out of college, standing in the middle of your twenties. Good decisions now mean you won't have a ton of baggage at your feet. But if you continue to listen to the voice of the good girl, you will still feel alone, worried you aren't doing enough, and bent over from the pressure that making all of those good decisions has left behind. You need more than a stack of good decisions, A+ papers, first place trophies, perfect attendance awards, and a list of right answers. You need life. You need freedom. *You need Jesus.*

Do you dare to stop trying so hard to live *for* God and believe that he asks you to live with him, *from* him? If you exist inside the safe place of Jesus, then you have been given everything you need for life. Do you believe it?

She Lives Fully

Sarah Masen was in town to do an outdoor concert at the baseball park. You have to know that she is one of my all-time favorite singer/songwriters. I had no ticket because in those early days of college, I didn't have the foresight to plan ahead for things like that. The driver's seat of my little black Corolla would be the best seat I would get, and I was okay with that. I drove to the park, determined to roll down the windows and find a spot on the street close to the stadium. I was happy there.

In the middle of "Come In," a couple leaving the concert early noticed me sitting small in the front seat behind my steering wheel, and the wife reached down deep into her pocket and pulled out an extra ticket. I hesitated at first, worried that maybe there was a catch. When I realized they really were offering me the ticket for free, I gratefully accepted, and within minutes, the gray muffled tones from the parking lot became rich and distinctly colorful. What had been background was now center stage.

I sat up front, counting her freckles. And then she came into the grassy area after her set, and I walked up to her. And we chatted, yes we did—about how her brother and I went to the same small school in a suburb of Detroit, though not at the same time; about how I remembered her before she was famous when she came to our youth group and sang folksy, poetic tunes from a stool in the front; about how I had been a fan ever since. I couldn't believe only an hour before I was content to sit in my car. Imagine all I would have missed!

But you know this isn't really about Sarah Masen. It's about how I'm living my life and how you're living yours.

Are you sitting on a side street listening to the concert from two blocks away?

Do you insist that you are okay with less when really you long for more?

Are you waiting for someone to give you permission to show up and be yourself with all of your quirks and giftedness and mess-ups and silliness?

Are you feeling left out, wondering when life is going to start for you?

Are you listening to the voices whispering untruths? Things like *Perform! Impress! Live up! Be perfect! Be right! Be the best! Earn your way in!*

Are you waiting for someone to come out of the concert and give you a free ticket inside?

I've got good news for you.

Someone already did.

You hide in your car because you think you're safe there, and Jesus walks up and bids you roll down your window. And when you do, he smiles that warm, rich, welcoming smile and extends his arm out toward you. When you question him with your eyes and shake your head no, he motions for you to come out of your car, and before you can stop yourself, you do. He stands there in front of you, stretches out his hand, and you take it because you can't not.

He walks with you toward the music and the action. Together you take thankful steps toward the center of adventure, and you realize you aren't so concerned about where you end up because you're with him. He doesn't promise there won't be trouble or hard times. He doesn't promise *easy*, but he does promise love. Fear may still creep in. But now, instead of trying to run and hide from the things you fear, he gives you the courage you need to face it. In fact, he doesn't just give you courage, he *is* your courage. Life isn't just about running *from something*, it's about running to Someone. *With Someone.* He speaks to you, and you know his voice because you know *him*. And even better? He knows you. As you learn to relate with Jesus personally, rules and religion pale in comparison to true, real, honest relationship.

You feel your shoulders begin to relax, that pain between your eyes starts to fade. That list of things you were worried about doesn't seem so long anymore. Your focus slowly shifts from the sight of your own feet and you lift up your head and are now able to see the faces of others. You know they are needy and hurting, but now you aren't moving toward them alone. Now you have Life walking with you, speaking to you, coming out of you, leading the way.

You don't care so much about being good.

You are simply thankful that he is.

And he lives in you, is with you, is here.

And your moments begin to feel a little less tense and a lot more graceful.

If he says he will do far more abundantly beyond what you could ask or think, then who are you to stop before he gets there? God is a God who begins and also finishes—he who began a good work in you will be faithful to complete it.

> Now to Him who is able to do far more abundantly beyond all that we ask or think, according to the power that works within us, to Him be the glory in the church and in Christ Jesus to all generations forever and ever. Amen. (Eph. 3:20–21)

finding your voice once you've been found

Questions for Further Reflection

Chapter 1 The Beginning

We all have ways we identify ourselves, labels we answer to whether or not we realize it: the responsible one, the smart one, the funny one, the ugly one, the indecisive one. What are some labels you've been wearing around?

What comes to mind when you hear the phrase *good girl*? Is it positive, negative, or a mix of both?

Would you agree that the best part of hiding is being found? Why or why not?

Chapter 2 The Girl Who Wears a Paper Face

At the beginning of the chapter, I share Kayla's story, a girl who desperately wanted to make sure she had everything worked out with God before she went off to college. What are some words to describe how Kayla was feeling?

In what areas of your life have you felt the pressure of perfection and to never make a mistake?

In this chapter we talk about how the opposite of fear is love. Do you agree or disagree with this statement?

Chapter 3 The Actress

In what ways can you relate with the Actress, the girl who hides behind her good performance?

In my own experience as an actress hiding behind my good performance, I believed this lie: *I have to perform to prove my worth.* Is there a statement you can identify that you believe? How does John 6:29 challenge that statement?

Chapter 4 The Girl Next Door

In what ways can you relate with the Girl Next Door?

Is there an Ashley Hall in your life, a girl with a great image but a bad reputation? How do you relate with her?

What is the difference between putting your confidence in your good decisions and putting your confidence in God?

Chapter 5 The Activist

In this chapter, Hannah travels to Uganda to spend time in an orphanage. When her friends announced they felt called back to Uganda, Hannah struggled. Can you understand this struggle Hannah had? Why or why not?

Have you ever felt like there are certain activities that are more Christian than others? Where did you get that idea?

Do you agree that sometimes it's easier to pick up a cause than to lay down your life? Why or why not? What is the difference between the two?

Chapter 6 The Heroine

Are you the responsible one among your group of friends? If so, how do you feel about that?

Do you struggle with taking responsibility for things unnecessarily? What kinds of things?

When your plans are interrupted, what is your first response?

Imagine yourself as Mary in Luke 1. There are several good girl voices listed on page 72. If you were Mary, which voice would have been most difficult for you to resist?

Chapter 7 The Bystander

Could you relate with Chloe, the girl who was looking for a safe place? What else do you think she was looking for?

What does living life on the sidelines look like for you? Can you think of a time when you know you were being asked to step away from the sidelines but you didn't? What about a time when you did?

In what ways have you experienced *El Roi*, "the God Who Sees"?

Chapter 8 The Judge

Why did God give the Ten Commandments?

When it comes to the rules, have you been a rule follower, a rule flexer, or a rule thrower-outer?

Jesus tells the crowd in John 6:29 that the work of God is to believe in the One he has sent. How do you feel about that statement? Does it feel too easy? Too hard?

After reading chapter 8, have any of your impressions changed about how God sees the rules?

Chapter 9 The Intellectual

Sometimes the best way to move past our fear is to look it straight in the eye. When it comes to school and grades, what is the worst thing that could happen to you?

In your opinion, what is the difference between caring about your grades and being obsessed with your grades?

Lucy was a girl who learned to cope with life by being the smartest girl in the room. Can you relate to Lucy at all? Why or why not?

What is the difference between being humbled before God and being humiliated in front of people?

Jesus asked his disciples, "Who do you say that I am?" How would you answer that question?

Chapter 10 The Dreamer

List some of the dreams you have for your future.

Are there certain dreams you are afraid to admit you have? Is there a part of you that is unwilling to admit some of the things you dream of for fear they are selfish or wrong or too unreasonable?

Consider the way you are made, your natural personality, the things you love to do—do you think of these things as gifts that God wants to develop, or are these things you've tried to hide?

Do you believe it's true that God can bring beauty out of the brokenness of life? Can you think of any times when you've seen proof of that?

Chapter 11 The Beloved

Do you understand the difference between feeling guilty and feeling ashamed? List out some characteristics of both.

For eleven chapters, we've talked about how listening to the voice of the good girl drives us into our hiding places. Listening to the voice of God drives us into a hiding place as well. What are the differences between hiding behind our good girl identities and having our lives hidden in Christ?

Chapter 12 The God Who Set Her Free

Describe someone who lives for God. What do they look like, sound like, feel like? How do you feel around them?

Consider this: describe someone who lives *from* God. Do you know anyone like that? Can you even tell the difference?

If the Sarah Masen concert represents life with God, where are you sitting?

from good to graceful

On the next page you will find a list of all of the voices we discussed in the book. Behind each voice, there is a fear, a right, and a hiding place. Holding on to your rights basically means anything you grip tightly in your hand and are unwilling to let go of. We hold on to certain things because we think our needs will be met by keeping them close. But God alone can meet these needs we so desperately have.

Each voice encourages us to seek safety in something other than God. For example, the voice of the Actress encourages us to seek our safety in our performances, so that is where we hide.

You may have different fears, rights, and hiding places associated with each voice and that's okay. The point is to get you thinking about how the voice of the good girl is not the voice of God. He speaks differently, offering love, truth, and a safe place to hide.

The Voice	Fears	Says	Holds on to	Hides behind	God says
Actress	She is inadequate.	*You have to perform.*	Her right to be successful.	Her performance.	*Even when you work hard, you can depend on me and I will do the work.* "But by the grace of God I am what I am, and His grace toward me did not prove vain; but I labored even more than all of them, yet not I, but the grace of God with me" (1 Cor. 15:10).
Girl Next Door	What people think.	*You have to impress.*	Her right to look good.	Her good reputation.	*I am the keeper of your reputation.* "For am I now seeking the favor of men, or of God? Or am I striving to please men? If I were still trying to please men, I would not be a bond-servant of Christ" (Gal. 1:10).
Activist	She won't make a difference.	*You have to make an impact.*	Her right to be important.	Her causes.	*Your importance comes from me.* "Not that we are adequate in ourselves to consider anything as coming from ourselves, but our adequacy is from God" (2 Cor. 3:5).
Heroine	Weakness.	*You have to be strong, responsible.*	Her right to be in control.	Her strength and responsibility.	*Your weakness is a beautiful opportunity for my strength.* "My grace is sufficient for you, for power is perfected in weakness" (2 Cor. 12:9).
Bystander	Exposure.	*You don't matter.*	Her right to be left alone.	Her comfort zone.	*Though the world may be confusing and unknown to you, you are known to me. I see you. I understand you fully.* "You know when I sit down and when I rise up; You understand my thought from afar" (Ps. 139:2).
Judge	Failure.	*You have to be perfect.*	Her right to be right.	Her rules.	*Simply believe me. I am well pleased with you. Period.* "This is the work of God, that you believe in Him whom He has sent" (John 6:29).
Intellectual	Criticism.	*You have to be the best.*	Her right to have the answers.	Her report card.	*Your critics and your competitors are not the ones who define you.* "Therefore humble yourselves under the mighty hand of God, that He may exalt you at the proper time, casting all your anxiety on Him, because He cares for you." (1 Peter 5:6-7).
Dreamer	She is missing out.	*Your life won't start until later.*	Her right to be happy.	Her somedays.	*Your dreams are safe in my hands.* "For I know the plans I have for you,' declares the LORD, 'plans for welfare and not for calamity to give you a future and a hope" (Jer. 29:11).

notes

Chapter 4 The Girl Next Door

1. Parker J. Palmer, *Let Your Life Speak* (San Francisco: Jossey-Bass, 2000), 9.

2. Want to find out who your celebrity look-alike is? Upload your photo to this site. It might be a man. Don't say I didn't warn you. http://celebrity.myheritage.com/face-recognition.

3. David Seamands, *Healing for Damaged Emotions* (Colorado Springs: NavPress, 2004), 24.

4. Fil Anderson, *Breaking the Rules* (Downers Grove, IL: InterVarsity, 2010), 47.

Chapter 6 The Heroine

1. *Merriam-Webster Online*, s.v. "responsible," accessed July 15, 2010, http://www.merriam-webster.com/dictionary/responsible.

2. Brennan Manning, *Reflections for Ragamuffins*, 1st ed. (New York: HarperSanFrancisco, 1998), 317.

Chapter 7 The Bystander

1. Holly Gerth, *God's Heart for You* (Eugene, OR: Harvest House, 2011), 91.

Chapter 9 The Intellectual

1. Quoted in Everett L. Worthington Jr., "The Paradox of Humility," accessed November 16, 2011, http://www.somareview.com/paradoxofhumility.cfm.

Chapter 10 The Dreamer

1. Sam McLoughlin, "A Cruise Ship Story," *The Default Life* (blog), April 8, 2011, http://www.thedefaultlife.com/popculture/a-cruise-ship-story/.

2. John Eldredge, *Desire* (Nashville: Thomas Nelson, 2007), 100.

Chapter 11 The Beloved

1. Zora Neale Hurston. BrainyQuote.com, Xplore Inc, 2011. http://www.brainyquote.com/quotes/quotes/z/zoranealeh106544.html, accessed July 16, 2011.

2. *Biblos*, s.v. "Colossians 3:15," accessed April 22, 2010, http://biblelexicon.org/colossians/3-15.htm.

3. *Merriam-Webster Online*, s.v. "umpire," accessed April 22, 2010, http://www.merriam-webster.com/dictionary/umpire.

Chapter 12 The God Who Set Her Free

1. Ruth Haley Barton, *Invitation to Solitude and Silence* (Downers Grove, IL: InterVarsity, 2004), 60.

2. Sarah Young, *Jesus Calling: A 365-Day Journaling Devotional* (Nashville: Thomas Nelson, 2010), 41.

3. Annie Downs, *Perfectly Unique* (Grand Rapids: Zondervan, 2012),

Acknowledgments

Big things are nearly always born small. This book started as the most inconsequential conversation in the café of our youth room in the fall of 2008. My friend and fellow youth leader Kendra and I overheard a conversation between two high school girls about school. It wasn't an earth-shattering, drama-filled confrontation. It was simply a casual exchange about a class they both had and their teacher's opinion of them. But Kendra and I both noticed the same thing as we listened – *these girls were desperate to please their teacher, to not be a disappointment, to be good*. And these girls reminded us of, well . . . *us*.

That was the first of many conversations Kendra and I had about what we jokingly named *the good girl syndrome*—but the name fit so well that it stuck. A few months later, Kendra and I hosted the first of three mini-retreats for the girls in our youth group who struggled with the voice of the good girl in their heads and longed to know there was more to living the Christian life than simply trying to be good.

This book would not exist without Kendra Adachi and the girls from Westover Church who attended those mini-retreats, The Good Girl Project in 2009, 2010, and 2012. Your honest stories paved the way for thousands of girls to live gracefully. And Kendra, thank you for being my person,

I want to also thank the girls in my small group, now seniors—Alicia Rouche, Brandy Buxton, Brooke Turnamian, Elizabeth Grady, Emma Peterson, Mary Catherine Hennigan, Mary Claire Brogden, Meredith Park, Olivia Kirkman, and Shannon Paylor—thank you for reading bits of this book when it was still just an idea. You are welcome at my house for Sunday night dinner from now until forever.

To current and former students in the Westover High School Ministry, especially Anna Howell, Christin Lane, and Julianna Royer, because you made it through high school battling the good girl and have lived to tell about it.

Thank you to friends who have cheered and supported the writing of this book—Alisa and Jason Windsor, for sharing your opinions, ideas, and talents; Melissa Lewkowicz, for always asking and believing; our small group, Dianne and Billy Stone and Kaz and Kendra Adachi, for praying, listening, and standing beside us; Lee and Stacey Williams, for bringing dinner, sharing ice cream, and loving us well; Annie Downs, for serving high school girls together with me and always being one text away from an encouraging word; Holley Gerth and Stephanie Bryant, for chasing your dreams and bringing me with you.

A special thanks to Bre Lillie for being the first high school girl to read these words. Your valuable feedback was so appreciated—thank you for your willingness.

To my writing group, The Thinklings, your encouragement, prayers, and writing advice were a safe place at the most important times. Thank you for being graceful.

To the faithful readers of my blog, Chatting at the Sky, as well as the writers and readers of (in)courage—I'm not sure you know how you have lifted me. Thank you for your bravery, your kindness, and your art.

To the entire publishing team at Revell—I admire your wisdom, professionalism, and respect for this message. Thank you for understanding those of us who struggle with the good girl and for helping to build the platform for her to find her voice.

Finally, to my family—our children who have been patient while I've finished this book, Daddy and I are so proud of you just because you belong to us. To the Freemans, Morlands, Smiths, and Kreges—thank you for your constant support, payers, movie nights, encouragement, babysitting, meals, and love. A special thanks to Myquillyn for putting up with having a tattletale little sister who always got you in trouble. You are a gift, sister girl.

And to my husband, John, I simply want to say in public and in print that it is an honor and a joy to watch Christ in you come out. Thank you for not rolling your eyes at me when we first got married when my good girl freaked out over not knowing what color to paint our living room wall. I look up to you, respect you, and can't wait to see what is to come.

It seems strange to thank Jesus here at the end, because in a very real way, thanking all of these people *is* thanking Jesus—I know they are all gifts straight from his hand. Still, your grace is too much for us, and you, Jesus, are remarkably more than I could have ever imagined. "Thank you" is too small, but I say it anyway.

Emily Freeman is a writer who loves to read and a speaker who would rather listen. Author of *Grace for the Good Girl: Letting Go of the Try-Hard Life*, she also writes for DaySpring (a division of Hallmark) and has traveled as a writer with Compassion International. She attended Columbia International University to study the Bible and the University of North Carolina at Greensboro where she earned a degree in Educational Interpreting for the Deaf. She is married to John, a student ministries pastor, and together they live in North Carolina with their three children.

Emily extends a daily invitation on her blog for women to create space for their souls to breathe. Come join the community of grace dwellers at www.ChattingAtTheSky.com.

People tell me that high school girls don't really read books. They say you are too busy texting people and looking in mirrors and stuff. I know you text people and look in mirrors from time to time. But even though I don't know you personally, I think I at least know this: You think deeply. You love hard. You care about things that I didn't care about when I was your age. And that's a good thing.

I also think you might be under a lot of pressure. School weighs heavy, expectations stare you in the face from every direction, and you struggle through issues and worries and relationships that might shock the adults in your life.

This book will not give you all the answers. But it is my most heartfelt hope that the words in this book will do one thing well: remind you that Jesus is present when people are broken.

Learning to live life gracefully may actually look pretty messy. It will be hard to figure out what you believe and then stand up for it. It will hurt when people misunderstand you. It might feel scary to trust an invisible God.

Graceful, in this case, doesn't mean perfect. Instead, it means free. Free to believe Jesus rather than that voice in your head that says you aren't good enough. Free to hope even when things look and feel hopeless. Free to embrace the truth that no matter what, if you have received Jesus, then he has received you. And you are marked forever by his divine grace. Not because you're good, but because he is.

Do you believe it?

I would love to hear from you.
Feel free to connect with me on 🅱 *emilypfreeman* or on my blog, *ChattingAtTheSky.com.*

May grace surprise you kindly,

Emily

"EMILY FREEMAN is one of those rare writers: profoundly biblical, lyrical, transparent—memorable. Her emancipating words on these pages offer the needed keys to all the good girls longing to take wing—and soar home to God's heart."

—ANN VOSKAMP, *New York Times* bestselling author of *One Thousand Gifts*

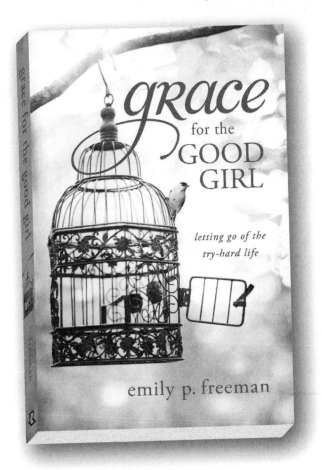

grace
for the
GOOD
GIRL

*letting go of the
try-hard life*

emily p. freeman

Revell
a division of Baker Publishing Group
www.RevellBooks.com